D1117594

The Urbana Free Library

To renew materials call
217-367-4057

X

DATE DUE		
~~JAN 27 2006~~	~~AUG 06 2006~~	
~~OCT 27 2006~~	~~MAY 31 2007~~	
~~MAY 28 2013~~	~~MAY 15 2008~~	
	~~APR 29 2009~~	
	~~MAY 27 2009~~	
	JUL 03 2012	

DISCARDED BY THE
URBANA FREE LIBRARY

ALAN DUNN'S

Exotic
SUGAR FLOWERS
for cakes

ALAN DUNN'S

Exotic
SUGAR FLOWERS
for cakes

URBANA FREE LIBRARY

MEREHURST

202 2495

Contents

Dedication

With love to Alice Christie, and to my parents,
Allen and Avril, and sister Sue.

Introduction

I was delighted to be asked to write a book on the subject of exotic flowers! In the past I have been able to incorporate some exotic flowers in my books, but I now have the opportunity to concentrate and use many of my favourite flowers, both in arrangements and for cake designs. I am interested in, and passionate about, a large range of plants, but it is the more unusual and exotic that I find most appealing.

I have tried to use a varied selection of flowers and foliage in this book in the hope that they may be of interest to a wide spectrum of cake decorators – it is difficult to know what will appeal to other people! I am often told that it is difficult to persuade customers to have exotic flowers on their cakes so, with this in mind I have included some designs that combine exotic flowers with the ever-popular rose!

◆

Interestingly, many flowers that are taken for granted and are considered to be 'normal' are actually exotic. It is because they are widely cultivated in Britain, or are sold by florists in large quantities, that they are now accepted as the norm. Flowers like freesias, snapdragons, nasturtiums, tulips and even the very familiar rose, all have exotic origins.

It is now easier than ever to buy exotic plants and flowers from garden centres, specialist nurseries and flower shops – so it seems a natural progression to make, and include, them in sugarcraft design. Some of the flowers and foliage featured in this book can be reasonably quick and simple to make, but there are others that are both challenging and time-consuming. It is important to choose carefully (and charge accordingly) if you are asked to include these flowers in your designs. I usually use large quantities of flowers on cakes to create impact, but it is not always necessary to do this when re-creating exotic flowers as they are often detailed enough to be used individually.

Although it is not always possible, I do try to copy fresh flowers. I usually either dissect, draw or photocopy the various sections of the flower for use as reference at a later date. It is also a useful means of studying and understanding how a flower should be made, formed, and coloured. However, some of the plants used in this book have been made using photographs and botanical illustrations, as a few of them were not available as cut flowers or were out of season when I needed to make them! It is often necessary to use artistic licence when making sugar flowers to speed up the process, anyway. This also helps to create character and sometimes improves on Mother Nature! Generally, it is better to develop the character of a plant or flower than simply to strive for botanical correctness. In other words, it is more important to add soul to your work than to make very neat, sterile flowers.

◆

As with my previous books, the cakes and floral arrangements pictured have been made as suggestions. It is important that you use this book only as a reference, adding your own interpretation and style to create your personal designs. Have fun!

Bower of Beauty Birthday Cake

This pretty birthday cake is a perfect example of how to use a very simple plant in a straightforward way to achieve stunning results. As you can see, sometimes it is just enough to allow the flowers to tell their own story! The heart-shaped cake has been slightly sculpted at the point to create a gently flowing design.

cake & decoration

17.5cm (7in) heart-shaped rich fruit cake
Apricot glaze
500g (1lb) white almond paste (marzipan)
Clear alcohol (kirsch, white rum, cointreau etc)
1.25kg (2½lb) white sugarpaste (rolled fondant)
Broad velvet magenta ribbon to trim the cake board
Deep magenta tubular ribbon to trim the base of the cake
Small amount of royal icing or flower paste (gum paste)
Non-toxic glue stick
Vine green and holly/ivy dusting powders (petal dust/blossom tint)

◆

equipment

Sharp knife
Sugarpaste smoothers
25cm (10in) heart-shaped cake board
2 cake picks

◆

flowers

12 bower of beauty flowers,
22 sets of foliage and
10 sets of buds (see p.10)

preparation

1 Use a sharp knife to cut and sculpt the cake into a curved, rounded heart. (One of the privileges of cake decorating is that you can always eat the off-cuts!) Brush the cake with apricot glaze and cover with almond paste. Allow to dry overnight. Moisten the surface of the almond paste with clear alcohol and cover with white sugarpaste. Use a combination of smoothers and a pad of softened paste pressed into your palm to smooth out the surface and edges of the cake.

2 Cover the heart-shaped cake board with white sugarpaste and position the cake on top. Again using the sugarpaste smoothers, try to form a neat join between the cake and the board. Leave the sugarpaste aside until completely dry.

3 Glue a band of broad velvet magenta ribbon to the edge of the board using a non-toxic glue stick. Carefully attach a band of deep magenta tubular ribbon to the base of the cake using either royal icing or some softened flower paste to hold it in position.

assembly

4 Wire the flowers, buds and foliage to create an informal reversed 'S'-shaped spray and also a smaller corsage to use at the base of the cake. Insert both sprays into cake picks and then into the cake.

5 Finally, dust the cake gently around the outline of both sprays. To do this, use a medium-sized flat dusting brush with a mixture of vine green and holly/ivy dusting powders.

Bower of Beauty

(Pandorea jasminoides)

One of eight species that are indigenous to Australia, *Pandorea jasminoides* has been cultivated to produce an attractive garden plant. Another of the species, *Pandorea pandorana*, although less attractive to my eye has a very appealing common name – wonga-wonga vine! The bower of beauty is a simple yet extremely effective flower for both the novice and experienced sugarcrafter to make. There are pure white, cream and pink cultivars with bright to dark pink throats, pure white forms and also cultivars with variegated foliage.

materials

30-, 28-, 26- and 20-gauge white wire
White or pale pink, and mid-holly/ivy flower paste (gum paste)
Aubergine, vine, holly/ivy and forest green dusting powders (petal dust/blossom tint)
Deep magenta craft dust
Nile green floristry tape
½ glaze

◆

equipment

Fine-nosed pliers and wire cutters
Celstick or ceramic tool
Five-petalled blossom cutter [OPF8] or similar
Silk veining tool
Fine sharp scissors
Tea rose leaf veiner [GI]

flowers

1 Cut several lengths of 26-gauge wire into quarters. Bend a hook in the end of each short length using pliers. Knead some white or pale pink paste until very pliable, form into a ball and then into a teardrop shape.

Pinch out the broad end of the teardrop between your finger and thumb to form a pedestal. Put the flat base of the pedestal against the board and roll out the base finely using a celstick. The area around the base of the back of the flower needs to be neat in order to use the cutter specified – if the paste is too thick you will find that the flower gets stuck in the hole of the cutter. Place the blossom cutter over the thick part of the pedestal and cut out the flower shape.

2 Elongate three of the petals by rolling them with a celstick to form the base of the flower. Open up the throat of the flower using the pointed end of the celstick. Put the flower on the side of your index finger (a smear of white fat might be needed to stop the flower sticking) and vein each petal using the silk veining tool. Increase the pressure at the edge of each petal to frill them slightly.

3 Moisten the hook on a length of 26-gauge wire and thread the wire carefully through the centre of the flower. You will probably be able to see the hook at the centre of the flower; if this does happen, simply plug up the hole with a small ball of flower paste. Push the paste into position with the rounded end of a celstick or ceramic tool.

4 Rest the three elongated petals against a flat surface and gently tilt the two top petals back slightly. Repeat this process to make the number of flowers that you require.

buds

5 The buds are very quick to make and help to create a gentle starting point when used in sprays and bouquets. To make them, form a ball of white flower paste into a sharp, pointed cone. Insert a dry 28-gauge wire into the broad end.

Hold the base of the cone firmly between your finger and thumb and then gradually thin down the bud using a rubbing action. The tip of the bud should remain in a sharp point.

6 Use your finger and thumb to pinch three petals from the top section of the bud. Next, twist the petals around in one direction to give the impression of a bud about to pop open.

leaves

7 The leaves grow in sets of five, seven and nine in the same way as those of the jasmine family. Form a teardrop-shaped piece of mid-holly/ivy, well-kneaded flower paste and insert a piece of moistened 30- or 28-gauge white wire. Place the wired teardrop against the workboard. Use the flat side of any rubber veiner to flatten the shape, to make it finer and to form the basic leaf shape. If the shape is a touch distorted, simply trim it into shape with a small pair of fine scissors.

8 Vein the leaf using a rose leaf veiner. Soften the edges by using the rounded end of a celstick. Pinch the leaf from the base along to the tip, to help create a natural shape.

Repeat this process to create plenty of leaves. For each set you will need one large leaf together with a few smaller leaves.

colouring & assembly

9 Dust the centre of each flower with a mixture of deep magenta and aubergine. Dust the calyces on both the flowers and buds with a mixture of vine and holly/ivy dusting powders.

10 Tape the leaves together using quarter width nile green tape. Begin with a large leaf and then tape the others down the stem in pairs. Dust the upper surface of each leaf with forest green, vine and holly/ivy dusting powders. Dip into a ½ glaze, shake off the excess and allow to dry.

11 Tape the buds and flowers into small clusters, and then tape them, along with the leaves, on to a piece of 20-gauge wire to form a trailing stem. The leaves should be added every time a group of flowers or buds are taped on to the stem. They should also be added in sets of two, as leaf axils emerging from the main stem.

Elegant and Exotic Wedding Cake

This elegant ivory wedding cake was designed for my cousin Sarah's wedding in May. She carried only white roses and dark green foliage in her bouquet, but I suggested using white bower of beauty flowers and dark green philodendron leaves along with the roses so that I could include her cake in this book! As you can see, the final result was really very stylish.

cake & decoration

15cm (6in) heart-shaped polystyrene dummy cake

Clear alcohol (kirsch, white rum, cointreau etc)

4.5kg (9lb) champagne sugarpaste (rolled fondant)

22.5cm (9in) and 30cm (12in) round-shaped rich fruit cakes

Apricot glaze

2.3kg (5lb) white almond paste (marzipan)

Small amount of royal icing

Fine gold ribbon to trim the base of the cakes

Broad gold-edged ivory organza-style ribbon to trim the edge of the board

15mm (½in) gold-edged ivory ribbon

Non-toxic glue stick

◆

equipment

Sugarpaste smoothers

22.5cm (9in) thin cake board and 40cm (16in) round cake board

Perspex tilting cake separator [C]

2 long crystal pillars [W]

Inexpensive sharp knife

Posy pick [W]

◆

flowers

3 Elegant and Exotic Wedding Sprays (see p.14)

preparation

I The top tier of this cake is made of polystyrene, which makes positioning it at an angle much easier. Moisten the polystyrene cake with clear alcohol and cover with champagne sugarpaste, using smoothers to achieve a good finish. Allow to dry for a few days.

2 Place the 22.5cm (9in) cake on the thin board and brush with apricot glaze. Cover the cake and board with white almond paste. Repeat the process with the base tier but without a board. Allow to dry for about a week.

Moisten the surface of the almond paste with clear alcohol and cover both cakes with champagne sugarpaste. Cover the base cake board with sugarpaste and transfer the larger cake on top. Put the 22.5cm (9in) cake on top of the 30cm

(12in) base tier and bond the two together by simply applying pressure with a sugarpaste smoother to the top of the smaller cake. Allow to dry.

3 Attach a band of fine gold ribbon around the base of all three cakes using a tiny amount of royal icing. Glue a length of ivory ribbon to the board edge using a non-toxic glue stick.

assembly

4 Place the heart-shaped cake on the tilting cake separator. Insert the perspex pins (provided with the stand) into the polystyrene through the holes provided in the stand. Put the stand and cake on top of the middle tier.

5 Wire up the three sprays of varying sizes as instructed on page 14. Insert the two larger sprays into the two long crystal pillars – which act as alternatives to cake picks. However, the pillars need slightly shortening first. To do this, heat the knife until red hot and then cut the tapered end of each pillar to the required length. Insert the flowers into the pillars and then insert them into the top and base tiers.

The smaller spray is inserted into the posy pick and then into the cake. Add two trailing lengths of ivory organza ribbon to the display and drape them attractively around the cake and flowers.

Elegant and Exotic Wedding Spray

The three sprays used on the Elegant and Exotic Wedding Cake on page 12 have all been wired up using the same technique, but the number of flowers and leaves varies. Here, the white bower of beauty makes a pleasant alternative as a filler flower or even as a main flower in bridal bouquets without being obviously exotic.

flowers

2 stems of white bower of beauty
plus a few extra flowers (see p.10)
1 full rose, 3 half roses and 3 buds (see
p.136 of *Floral Wedding Cakes & Sprays*)
5 philodendron leaves (see p.25)

◆

equipment

20-gauge wire
Fine-nosed pliers
Wire cutters
Nile green floristry tape
A few gold-trimmed ivory organza
ribbon loops

preparation

1 Strengthen any flower and leaf stems by taping 20-gauge wire on to them.

assembly

2 To form the start of the spray and the basic outline, bend the ends of two stems of bower of beauty at an angle of 90 degrees, and tape them together using half width nile green floristry tape. Trim away the excess wire.

3 Tape the full rose into the centre of the spray to form the focal point. Add the three half roses around the central flower and tape them in tightly. Add the rose buds to the outer points of the spray and trim off any excess wire.

4 Begin to add depth to the spray by adding the philodendron leaves to the large gaps in the spray at this stage.

5 Fill in the remaining gaps with individual bower of beauty flowers, buds and leaves. Add some large ribbon loops at the same time. Trim off the excess wire and neaten the handle by taping over with the floristry tape.

Orchid Fever Cake

These stunning white and magenta miltoniopsis orchids are the focal flowers on this single-tiered wedding cake. They have been complemented with variegated and magenta South Sea Island ti leaves and the unusual lime green, blue and pink flowers of Queen's tears. The flowers and foliage on this cake are all very time-consuming to make, so it is not necessary to add decoration to the sides of the cake.

cake & decoration

25cm (10in) elliptical-shaped rich fruit cake
Apricot glaze
1.25kg (2½lb) white almond paste
(marzipan)
Clear alcohol (kirsch, white rum,
cointreau etc)
2kg (4lb) white sugarpaste (rolled fondant)
Small amount of royal icing
Fine white satin ribbon to trim the base of
the cake
15mm (½in) magenta velvet ribbon to trim
the edge of the cake board
Non-toxic glue stick

◆

equipment

Sugarpaste smoothers
36cm (14in) elliptical-shaped cake board
Celpick
Posy pick [W]
Fine-nosed pliers
Wire cutters

◆

flowers

Orchid Fever Spray (see p.18)
Small spray comprising:
1 miltoniopsis orchid and bud stem
(see p.22)
1 stem of Queen's tears (see p.28)
12 South Sea Island ti leaves (see p.26)

preparation

1 Brush the cake with apricot glaze and cover the surface with white almond paste. Leave the cake to dry for several hours, preferably overnight.
Moisten the surface of the paste with clear alcohol and cover with white sugarpaste. Use the sugarpaste smoothers to create a good, even finish. Cover the board with white sugarpaste and transfer the cake on top. Use the smoothers again to smooth and ease the paste around the base of the cake. There should be a neat bond between the board and the cake.

2 Attach a double band of white satin braid around the base of the cake. Glue a length of magenta velvet ribbon to the edge of the board using the non-toxic glue stick.

assembly

3 Wire up the spray of flowers as described on page 18, then form a smaller corsage to sit at the base of the cake. Insert the small corsage into the celpick and then into the base of the cake. Insert the larger spray into the posy pick and position this in the top of the cake.
When the cake is finished, you may need to stand back at a distance, in order to check for any adjustments and to ensure that the final display is suitably balanced.

Orchid Fever Spray

This eye-catching combination of flowers was chosen to create a flamboyant, fun and fresh design. It is unusual for me to create a spray of flowers without lots of green foliage, but this one works particularly well. The spray could be displayed in an attractive container after the celebration, but the flowers should be kept in a fairly dark and dry environment if they are to survive for a long period of time.

flowers

3 stems of Queen's tears (see p.28)
2 miltoniopsis orchids (see p.22)
3 stems of orchid buds (see p.24)
5 small groups of South Sea Island
ti leaves (see p.26)

◆

equipment

Wire cutters
Fine-nosed pliers
Nile green floristry tape
Tall wavy glass bottle

assembly

1 Begin the spray by forming the basic outline. To do this, bend the ends of the three stems of Queen's tears at an angle of 90 degrees, making the side stem slightly shorter in length. Tape the three pieces together using half width nile green floristry tape. Trim away the excess wires with the fine-nosed pliers. Tape in the three stems of orchid buds.

2 Create the focal point for the spray by using the two miltoniopsis orchids. Ensure that one of the flowers is slightly higher at the very heart of the spray. The faces of the flowers should be positioned so that they are not all pointing in the same direction.

3 Finally, tape in the various groups of South Sea Island ti leaves to fill in the gaps. Trim away any excess wire and then neaten the handle of the spray by taping over it with a piece of full width floristry tape. Adjust any of the flowers as necessary.

Orchid Fever Arrangement

This unusual orchid arrangement includes two varieties of pink miltoniopsis orchid, accompanied by variegated South Sea Island ti leaves and hanging Queen's tears flowers. Philodendron leaves have been used to create more depth in the arrangement and to help balance the darker orchids with the brightness of other components.

flowers

3 miltoniopsis orchids and 3 stems of buds (see p.22)
4 stems of Queen's tears (see p.28)
7 sets of assorted South Sea Island ti leaves (see p.26)
7 philodendron leaves (see p.25)

◆

equipment

Non-toxic glue
Florist's green staysoft or small block of oasis
Small green glass dish
Fine-nosed pliers
Several pink ribbon loops

preparation

1 Apply a small amount of non-toxic glue to a ball of florists' staysoft or oasis and position it in the centre of the green glass dish. Remember to allow the glue to set thoroughly before arranging the flowers.

assembly

2 Hook the ends of each of the miltoniopsis orchid stems, Queen's tears and orchid bud stems – this will help to support each of the flowers. Insert the three orchid flowers into the staysoft so that they form a diagonal line. Make sure that they all face in slightly different directions. Add the three orchid bud stems to form the basic shape of the arrangement.

3 Add the hanging stems of Queen's tears to extend the size of the arrangement and define its shape. Hook the ends of each of the South Sea Island ti leaf crowns and then fill in the spaces around the orchids, trying to balance the colours as you work. Use pliers to insert some clumps deep into the arrangement.

4 Finally, add the philodendron leaves around the edge of the arrangement, again hooking each of the stems for extra support. Adjust and relax the flowers and foliage into place. I have used several ribbon loops to fill in the back and the centre. However, if you are planning to enter a competition you must check the schedule to make sure that ribbon loops are allowed!

Miltoniopsis Orchid

Miltoniopsis orchids are hybrids of the miltonia orchid, which originate from South America. They are often commonly known as the pansy orchids because of their characteristic heart-shaped throat petal and face-like markings. The flowers have a very velvety texture, which is particularly difficult to achieve in sugar and often produce a very sweet scent at night that can be overpowering if kept in a bedroom. The colour ranges from white, pink, magenta and red, to burgundy and creamy yellow flowers. The plant that I used as my inspiration had two sizes of flower on it – I have used the smaller size but have provided the larger petal templates at the back of the book.

materials

28-, 24- and 18-gauge white wire
White flower paste (gum paste)
Primrose, lemon
and vine green dusting powders
(petal dust/blossom tint)
Deep magenta craft dust
Isopropyl alcohol
Nile green floristry tape

◆

equipment

Ceramic silk veining tool [HP]
Sharp scalpel and fine scissors
Petal templates (see p.151)
Plain edge cutting wheel [PME]
Medium ball tool

column

1 Bend a small hook in the end of a 28-gauge wire. Roll a very small piece of white paste into a ball and then into a cone shape. Insert the moistened, hooked wire into the fine end.

   Hollow out the upper part of the column using the rounded end of the ceramic silk veining tool (or something similar). Use a fine pair of scissors to make two tiny cuts into the top of the column. Pinch each cut section and curl them forward. The curved pieces will represent the anther cap. Put the paste aside for a few hours to dry.

throat petal

2 Roll out some white flower paste with a small rolling pin, leaving a ridge at the centre of the petal to insert the wire. Place the throat petal template on top of the paste and cut out the petal shape using a sharp scalpel.

3 Insert a moistened 24-gauge white wire into the thick ridge. At the top of the petal there are two points – these will need to be pinched and thinned down slightly.

4 Vein the surface of the petal in a fan formation using the silk veining tool. (Be very gentle as the orchid is not heavily veined.) Soften the edges of the petal and again frill gently using the silk veining tool.

5 Pinch a subtle central ridge along the top of the petal with your finger and thumb. Allow the paste to firm up slightly before colouring – the petal should be dried flat with only a small amount of movement around the edges.

lateral petals (wings/arms)

6 Roll out a small amount of white flower paste, leaving a thick ridge along the centre. Place the lateral petal template over the ridged paste and cut out the petal shape using a scalpel.

7 Insert a length of moistened 28-gauge white wire into the thick ridge. Position the petal on a pad and soften the edges with a medium ball tool. To vein the petal, try using the small wheel of the plain edge cutting wheel. However, do take care not to vein the petal too heavily, otherwise the tool will cut the paste.

   Draw a central vein down the paste before adding two or three smaller veins on either side. Pinch the petal at the base and at the tip. Repeat to make two lateral petals and allow to dry.

dorsal & lateral sepals (head & legs)

8 Repeat the above process using the dorsal and lateral sepal templates. The sepals should each have fewer veins on them. Allow to dry.

colouring & assembly

9 Dust a patch of primrose, mixed with lemon dusting powder, on to the upper part of the throat petal. The colouring takes the shape almost of a heart. Dust a very gentle border around the yellow using deep magenta craft dust.

10 Dilute a small amount of deep magenta craft dust with isopropyl alcohol and paint some fine line markings on the petal. If possible, use a photograph or real flower as a guide for the markings.

11 Dust a patch of deep magenta at the base of the two lateral petals and then a dash of primrose or lemon dusting powder on to the two lateral sepals. The lateral sepals of this orchid have some painted deep magenta streaks next to the yellow colouring.

12 Tape the column tightly into the centre of the pointed section of the throat petal shape using half width nile green floristry tape. Next, tape the two wing petals on either side of the column. Add the head and legs behind the wing petals. Dust the back and the tips of the flower lightly with vine green powder.

buds

13 These are very slender, gracefully shaped buds and are ideal for filling space. To make them, roll a ball of white flower paste into a slende,r teardrop shape. Insert a hooked 24-gauge wire into the broader end of the bud. Roll the bud between your finger and thumb to create a graceful curve.

Smooth the shape between your palms and divide the bud into three sections, using a sharp scalpel or cutting wheel. Make several buds in graduating sizes to complete a full stem.

assembly

14 Tape over each of the bud stems with half width nile green floristry tape. You will need to give the stems two or three layers of tape to thicken the stems sufficiently.

15 Tape the smallest bud on to the end of an 18-gauge wire. Continue down the stem, alternating the buds and increasing them in size. Tape in the flowers as required.

note

The plant produces long, strap-like leaves. These are not very attractive when made in sugar and it is generally preferable to use other, more delicate types of foliage to complement the main flower head.

Philodendron

Philodendrons are mostly from South America. The leaves vary quite a lot between the various species. The variety pictured here can produce very large leaves, however for most purposes the smaller leaves are easier to use in sugarcraft design.

materials

Dark green flower paste (gum paste)
20- and 18-gauge wire
Forest green, foliage green and aubergine dusting powders (petal dust/blossom tint)
½ glaze
Nile green floristry tape

◆

equipment

Leaf templates (see p.151)
Sharp scalpel
Medium ball tool
Philodendron leaf veiner [GI]
Bubblefoam sponge

2 Place the leaf template on top of the paste and cut out the leaf using a sharp scalpel. Insert a moistened 20- or 18-gauge wire into about half the length of the thick ridge.

3 Place the leaf on a pad and soften the edges using a medium ball tool. Put the leaf into the philodendron leaf veiner and press firmly to produce definite veins.

colouring

4 In order to achieve a strong, dark green colouring, the leaf needs to be dusted quite quickly after it is made. Begin by dusting aubergine around the edge of the leaf and then overdust heavily with foliage and forest greens. You may need to overdust this surface with some aubergine, in order to achieve a very dark leaf.

Allow the leaf to dry with a little movement to the edges, using bubblefoam sponge to support it.

5 Dip the leaf into a ½ glaze and allow to dry. Thicken the stems with floristry tape and, if necessary, add more 18-gauge wire to the main stem to support the weight of the leaf.

leaves

1 Although these leaves are smaller than most of those found on a philodendron plant, you will still need to use a large amount of paste for each leaf. Roll out some dark green flower paste, leaving a very thick ridge at the centre to allow a heavy gauge wire to be inserted.

25

South Sea Island Ti Leaf
(Cordyline *fruticosa*)

South Sea Island ti leaf is the most commonly cultivated ornamental cordyline. The leaves can be huge, but I have re-created them from two house plants I own that have fairly small leaves – the variety is called 'Red Edge'. These leaves make a wonderful addition to sprays and arrangements, almost creating the effect of individual flowers. The leaves are often called 'ti plant' by the floristry industry.

materials

Pale melon or mid-ruby flower paste
(gum paste)
26-, 24- and 18-gauge white wire
Forest green, holly/ivy, vine green and
purple dusting powders (petal dust/
blossom tint)
Deep magenta craft dust
Isopropyl alcohol
Nile green floristry tape
$\frac{1}{2}$ glaze

◆

equipment

Plain edge cutting wheel [PME]
or sharp scalpel
Foam pad
Large celstick
Tulip leaf veiner [GI]
Fine-nosed pliers and wire cutters

leaves

1 Roll out your chosen colour of
flower paste, leaving a thick ridge
down the centre. Cut out a basic leaf
shape using the large end of the plain
edge cutting wheel. Work the base of
the leaf between your finger and thumb
to leave a thickened stem.

2 Insert a moistened 24-gauge wire
into the thick ridge of the leaf. Place
the leaf on a pad and soften the edges
using the rounded end of the celstick.

3 Place the leaf into the tulip leaf
veiner and press firmly. Remove the

leaf from the veiner, place it back on
to a pad and draw down a central vein
using the cutting wheel. Take care not
to apply too much pressure because you
will cut the paste. Pinch the leaf from
the base to the tip, to accentuate the
central vein. Allow the leaf to dry with a
curve to the tip. Repeat this process to
make leaves of varying sizes.

4 At the top of the plant there is
usually one slightly unfurling leaf.
Roll out either pale melon or mid-ruby
coloured flower paste, leaving a thick
ridge at the centre of the leaf.
Cut out a freehand leaf shape using
the plain edge cutting wheel. Insert a
moistened 26-gauge wire into the thick
ridge and then place the leaf on a pad
and soften the edges slightly using the
rounded end of a celstick. Vein the leaf
as before and then apply a small amount
of egg white to one edge of the leaf and
then roll it up slightly. Curl the tip back.

colouring

5 Dust the pink leaves with deep
magenta craft dust and then
tinge the edges here and there
with purple dusting
powder. Dilute some
holly/ivy and forest
green powders
with isopropyl
alcohol and
paint some fine central
veining on to the smaller
leaves and large streaks

of colour on to the larger ones. Allow to
dry and dip into a $\frac{1}{2}$ glaze.

6 Mix together the vine green, forest
green and holly/ivy dusting powders.
Use this mix to add streaks to the pale
melon coloured leaves. Touch the edges
with deep magenta diluted with alcohol.
Use the same colour for the fine veins.
Try not to make the lines too neat, as
this will add to the natural appearance.
Glaze as before.

assembly

7 Tape the small unfurling leaf on
to the end of an 18-gauge wire.
Increase the size of the leaf as you
work down the stem. The leaves
should work all the way around the
stem to form shapes almost like crowns.
Dust the main stem with deep
magenta on the pink plant and holly/ivy
on the variegated plant.

Queen's Tears

(Billbergia nutans)

Billbergia nutans is part of the bromeliad family, which also includes the more popular pineapple plant. It is native to South America and Brazil, and is one of fifty species in the genus. The brightly coloured bracts can be pink, orange or red in colour, but the flowers always have this very unusual yet stunning combination of green flowers with blue edges and pink calyces.

materials

Pink or white, and nile green
floristry tape
33- and 20-gauge wire
Small lemon or white seed-head
stamens
Non-toxic high-tack craft glue
Egg white
Vine green, fuchsia, plum, primrose,
lemon, deep purple and
cornflower blue dusting powders
(petal dust/blossom tint)
Small amount of white flower paste
(gum paste)
Isopropyl alcohol

◆

equipment

Fine-nosed pliers
Wire cutters
Sharp scalpel
Flower templates (see p.151)
Plain edge cutting wheel [PME]
Foam pad
Dresden veining tool

stamens & pistil

1 Shred some full width nile green floristry tape into quarter width strips. Tape approximately 2.5cm (1in) of fine tape on to a short length of 33-gauge wire, leaving a flap at the end of the wire. Trim the flap and then cut the end into three sections. Twist or tweak each section to make them look finer – this represents the pistil. Dust with vine green dusting powder.

2 The stamens are actually T-bar shaped, but it can be time consuming to produce six hand-made stamens for each flower, so I opted to use commercial stamens. Glue six stamens on to the pistil using a tiny amount of non-toxic high-tack craft glue.
  Dust the filaments with vine green and the anthers with a mixture of primrose and lemon dusting powders. Attach a small piece of flower paste at the base of the stamens to act as padding for the three petals.

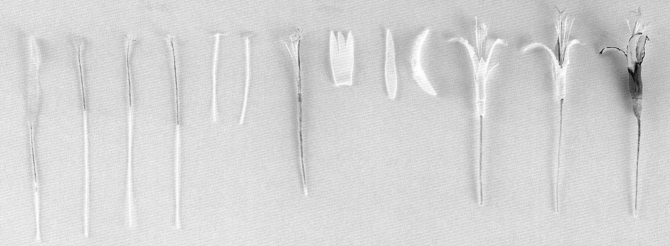

petals

3 Roll out some white flower paste and cut out three narrow petal shapes using the narrow orchid cutter. (The cutter used here was squashed to make it even slimmer!) Place the petals on a pad and soften the edges using the rounded end of a celpick. Draw down a central vein on each petal.

Moisten the base of each petal with egg white and attach to the padded paste on the stamens. Hang the flower until it has firmed up enough to curl the petals back slightly. Dust the petals with vine green dusting powder and allow to dry thoroughly.

You may prefer to actually wire each of the petals so that they are all well supported. However, bear in mind that this will make the whole process much more time consuming!

4 Paint the edges of each petal with a mixture of isopropyl alcohol, cornflower blue and deep purple dusting powders.

calyx

5 Roll out some more white flower paste, leaving a thick strip to one side of the paste. Put the calyx template (page 151) on top of the paste, with the base of the calyx on the thick strip. Cut out the shape using a sharp scalpel.

Put the calyx on a pad and soften the edges but do not frill the shape. Vein the centre of each of the sepals. Moisten the veined side of the calyx and wrap around the dried petals. Work the base of the calyx so as to hide the join. Squeeze a waistline between the sepals and the base of the calyx.

6 Dust the sepals with a mixture of fuchsia and plum dusting powders. Coat the base of the calyx with a bright vine green tint. Paint the tips of each of the sepals using the same deep purple/cornflower blue mixture as used for the edges of the petals. Tape over each of the stems using quarter width nile green tape.

bracts & assembly

7 Cut out several pointed bract shapes from full width pink or white floristry tape. Using the fine end of the dresden veining tool, vein the centre of each bract shape. (You will need to stretch the tape a little to give it a realistic bract shape.) Dust each bract heavily with fuchsia and plum powders.

8 Tape the flowers into groups of three or five and then tape them on to the end of a 20-gauge wire using white or pink tape. Add a long bract at the top of the stem and then add more down the stem. Dust the stem as for the bracts. Allow the flowers to hang with their heads down.

African Leaf Cake

Bird of paradise plants produce foliage that is far too large to reproduce easily in sugar. Therefore, I decided to make the cake in the shape of a leaf – it looks rather like a decorative, carved, wooden container. The floral arrangements include bird of paradise flowers, blue glory bower, fish-tail fern and philodendron foliage tinged with gold. The combination of colours, textures and shapes makes a striking display.

cake & decoration

30cm (12in) long-shaped rich fruit cake
Apricot glaze
1.5kg (3lb) white almond paste (marzipan)
Clear alcohol (kirsch, white rum,
cointreau etc)
2kg (4lb) white sugarpaste (rolled fondant)
coloured with holly/ivy paste food colour
Antique gold, light gold
and bronze metallic lustre dusts [SK]
Holly/ivy, forest green, foliage green
and vine green dusting powders
(petal dust/blossom tint)
Isopropyl alcohol
Green/blue iridescent ribbon
to trim the edge of the cake board
Non-toxic glue stick

◆

equipment

Sharp knife
Sugarpaste smoothers
40cm (16in) long board with rounded ends
Plain edge cutting wheel [PME]
Medium and large ball tools
Large flat paintbrush
Fine-nosed pliers and wire cutters

◆

flowers

2 bird of paradise flowers,
plus one extra set of petals and
1 bird of paradise leaf (see p.34)
3 stems of blue glory bower of varying
lengths (see p.40)
12 philodendron leaves (see p.25)
1 stem of fish-tail fern (see p.139)

preparation

1 Use a sharp knife to cut the fruit cake into the shape of a bird of paradise leaf – this will require some confidence, but it is not too difficult. (Keep the off-cuts of cake as these can be used to make a very rich version of bread and butter pudding!)

Next, brush the cake with apricot glaze and cover with almond paste. Allow the glaze to dry. Moisten the surface of the almond paste with clear alcohol and cover with the green sugarpaste. Cover the cake board with sugarpaste and then position the cake on top.

leaf design

2 To form the textured surface of the cake you will need to work quite quickly – otherwise the sugarpaste will start to dry and crust before you have finished. Begin by using the large end of the cutting wheel to form the central vein of the leaf. Use the medium and large ball tools in turn to stroke and stretch the paste into the shape of the deep veins.

Repeat the process on the side of the cake and the base board. Some areas of the design have been punched with the small end of the medium tool to create some background interest in the leaves.

3 Dust and overpaint the cake with forest green, vine, foliage and holly/ivy powders diluted with a small amount of isopropyl alcohol. Use a large, flat paintbrush and take care not to apply too much moisture, otherwise the cake will end up very sticky.

Allow the surface to dry, and then gild the edges and raised areas of the leaves with the three metallic lustre colours. You can use either a paintbrush or a finger!

4 Attach a band of broad green/blue iridescent ribbon to the edge of the board using a non-toxic glue stick.

assembly

5 Arrange the flowers as instructed on page 32 and wire together a small spray using a set of bird of paradise petals, a sprig of blue glory bower and three philodendron leaves. Position the large arrangement behind the cake and the small spray to the left of the design.

Bird of Paradise Arrangement

Bird of paradise flowers can be difficult to arrange with other species, but here I have used blue glory bower to pick up the blue already present in the main flora. If an arrangement is to be successful with these varieties, then you will need to use smaller, simply formed blooms to complement, rather than detract from, the focal flowers.

flowers

1 stem of fish-tail fern (see p.139)
Several philodendron leaves (see p.25)
3 stems of blue glory bower (see p.40)
2 bird of paradise flowers and one set of petals (see p.34)

◆

equipment

18-gauge wire
Nile green floristry tape
Gold spray paint
Black, shallow round dish
Florists' long pin holder
Florists' green staysoft or a small block of dry oasis
Fine-nosed pliers
Wire cutters

preparation

1 Strengthen the fish-tail fern, philodendron and blue glory bower leaves by adding 18-gauge wire alongside the main stems. Tape over with nile green floristry tape. Spray the foliage lightly with the decorative gold spray paint and allow to dry.

assembly

2 Place the pin holder on the dish and cover with green staysoft. Next, position the two large bird of paradise flowers in the staysoft so that they face in opposite directions.

3 Curve the three stems of blue glory bower gently and add to the arrangement in a line between the bird of paradise flowers. Add the single set of blue and orange petals to the base of the display. Position the fish-tail fern at the back and fill in the gaps, and add depth, with the philodendron leaves.

Bird of Paradise
(*Strelitzia reginae*)

Strelitzia reginae was named after Queen Charlotte Sophia, the daughter of the Duke of Mecklenburg-Strelitz in north Germany. It is strange that such a dramatic, majestic flower was named after Queen Charlotte, as she was reported to have been a rather dull and undistinguished woman, even though she was a dutiful wife to King George III. There are five species of *Strelitzia*, and all are native to South Africa. The flowers have become very popular among flower arrangers and florists alike, adding an immediate touch of the exotic to any floral display.

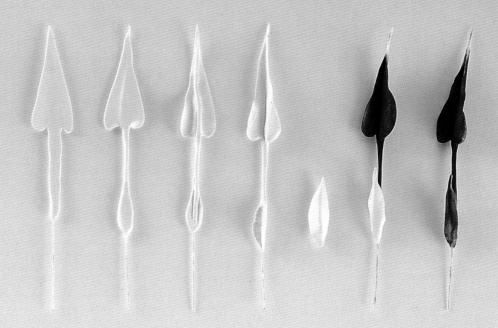

templates (see p.152)

materials

White and mid-green flower paste
(gum paste)
26-, 24-, 20-, 18- and 14-gauge
white wire
Egg white
Orange and purple craft dusts
Red, primrose, white, forest green,
holly/ivy, aubergine, plum, fuchsia
and vine green dusting powders
(petal dust/blossom tint)
¹/₂ or ³/₄ glaze
White floristry tape
Kitchen paper

◆

equipment

Stamen and flower
templates (see p.152)
Sharp scalpel
Foam pad
Dresden veining tool
Large and small ball tools
Plain edge cutting wheel [PME]
Dried sweetcorn husk veiner or
veiner no. 22 (Asi-és)
Fine-nosed pliers
Wire cutters
Fine-angled tweezers
Sharp scissors
Large flat paintbrush

stamens

1 The pointed blue stamens look very much like petals in this flower. It is best to make the stamens with white flower paste and then dust them to achieve both a density and brightness of colour. First, roll out some white flower paste, leaving a thick ridge at the centre for the wire. Place the stamen template on top of the paste and cut out the shape using a sharp scalpel. Insert a moistened 26-gauge white wire into the thick ridge, so that the wire goes into the top section of the shape.

2 Thin down the narrow part of the stamen, working the paste firmly between your finger and thumb. Place the stamen on a pad and soften the edges of the arrow head. Vein the centre of the arrow head and then pinch it firmly between your finger and thumb to emphasize the vein. Put the stamen, vein-side down, on to the pad and use a small ball tool to hollow out either side of the vein. This will help to shape the stamen more. Pinch the tip of the stamen into a fine, sharp point.

3 Roll out some white paste thinly and cut out the stamen bract shape. Soften the edges and attach to the base of the stamen with some egg white. Allow to firm a little. Repeat to make

the required number of stamens – there should be one stamen to every three orange petals.

colouring

4 Dust the stamen with purple craft dust, leaving the very base and the tip white. Dust the tip of the stamen heavily with white dusting powder to represent the pollen.

petals

5 There are two sizes of petal shape – you will need to make two large and one small for each section of the flower. Roll out some white flower paste, leaving a thick ridge at the centre. Place one of the petal templates on top of the paste and cut it out using the plain edge cutting wheel or a sharp scalpel.

Insert a moistened 24-gauge wire into the thick ridge and vein the petal on both sides with the sweetcorn husk veiner. Roll the base of the petal into a tube and then place the petal on a pad. Draw a central vein down the paste with the fine end of a dresden veining tool. Pinch the vein right to the tip to give the petal some shape. Repeat to make the required number of petals. (I usually use one or two sets of three per flower head, but there can be more.)

colouring & assembly

6 Dust the petals heavily on both sides with orange craft dust and then overdust with a touch of red powder. Allow to dry before dipping the petals in a ½ or ¾ glaze, depending upon how shiny you want the flowers to be.

7 Tape two large petals together, add a stamen and then a smaller petal underneath the stamen, using half width white floristry tape. Repeat the process until you have the total number of groups you require. Next, tape two or three groups together to the end of a 14-gauge wire using full width white tape. If you can see too much wire at the base of the petal groups, then you will need to apply some softened flower paste over the wires. Smooth the paste over the wires to make them blend into the main body of the petals.

8 To form the base of the 'beak', tape over a few 18-gauge wires and add to the main stem at an angle. Build up the beak using flower paste. Trim off the excess paste. Smooth some of this paste down on to the neck of the flower. Allow to dry. Thicken the rest of the stem with shredded kitchen paper, taped over with full width white tape.

large bract

9 Roll out a large piece of mid-green flower paste, though not too thinly. Cut out the bract shape freehand or use the template on page 152 as a guideline, using the plain edge cutting wheel. Vein gently with the no. 22 veiner. Moisten the bract with egg white and then cover the base paste on the beak. Carefully smooth the paste on to the beak and pinch the tip into a sharp point. Trim the upper edge of the bract with a pair of sharp scissors. Some of the bract shape should also be smoothed down to form the neck of the flower.

stem bracts

10 Roll out more paste and cut out some pointed bracts that are wide enough to wrap around the neck of the flower. Soften the edges and vein as for the large bract. Moisten and attach a long, pointed bract around the top of the neck. Trim off any excess paste. Repeat to cover the length of stem required for your arrangement.

colouring

11 Dust the upper edge of the bracts with primrose and vine green dusting powders. Overdust the very edges with a mixture of plum and fuchsia powders, then overdust again with aubergine powder. The main body of the beak and stem is dusted with forest green and holly/ivy. Overdust heavily with white; then steam.

leaves

12 The leaves are very large and leathery in texture. Roll out a large piece of mid-green flower paste, leaving a long thick ridge to take a heavy gauge wire. Cut out the leaf shape using the plain edge cutting wheel. Insert a moistened 20- or 18-gauge wire into the ridge. (The exact gauge will depend upon the size of the leaf.)

13 Place the leaf on a pad and soften the edges with a large ball tool. Use a pair of fine-angled tweezers to create the central vein in a ridge form. Turn the leaf over and vein the back of the leaf with the dresden veining tool, which should in turn leave raised veins on the front of the leaf. Turn the leaf over and hollow out the sections between the ridges with a ball tool. Allow to firm up a little before adding the colour.

colouring

14 Dust the edges, tip and base of the leaf with aubergine dusting powder. Dust the whole leaf heavily with holly/ivy and forest green. If more depth is required, add aubergine to a greater extent of the leaf.

Dip the leaf into a ½ glaze (a large container of glaze is required to do this) or paint with a large, flat paintbrush. The brush strokes should follow the direction of the veins on the leaf. Allow to dry and then highlight the central vein with some diluted white dusting powder. Overdust the central vein with a little green powder to remove the starkness from the white.

Blue and Green Grasshopper Cake

Grasshoppers are often used as good luck symbols. This small cake was intended as an alternative christening cake, but it could also be used to celebrate a birthday, new job or even a new house. The cake was very simple to decorate and is an ideal project for a novice sugarcrafter. The abstract rice paper grasshoppers were great fun to make!

cake & decoration

15cm (6in) scalloped, oval-shaped, rich fruit cake
Apricot glaze
400g (14oz) white almond paste (marzipan)
Clear alcohol (kirsch, white rum, cointreau etc)
500g (1lb) white sugarpaste (rolled fondant)
Small amount of royal icing
Fine Wedgwood blue or lilac ribbon to trim the edge of the cake base and board
Baby blue picot-edge ribbon to trim the edge of the cake board
Non-toxic glue stick
Lavender, bluebell, white and holly/ivy dusting powders (petal dust/blossom tint)
Rice paper
Cocoa butter

◆

equipment

Sugarpaste smoothers
25cm (10in) oval cake board
Grasshopper template (see p.153)
Fine pencil
Fine scissors
Fine paintbrushes
Mug and saucer
Celpick

◆

flowers

1 curved stem of blue glory bower (see p.40)

preparation

1 Brush the cake with warmed apricot glaze and cover with white almond paste. Allow to dry overnight. Moisten the surface of the almond paste with clear alcohol and cover with white sugarpaste, using a pair of sugarpaste smoothers to achieve a good finish.

Cover the board with sugarpaste and then position the cake on top, making sure that you have a neat join between both edges. Allow to dry.

2 Attach a fine band of Wedgwood blue or lilac ribbon around the base of the cake using a small amount of royal icing. Tie four bows, and attach one to each of the indents on the cake. Glue a band of baby blue picot-edge ribbon to the board and trim the edges with a finer band of Wedgwood blue ribbon.

side design

3 Use a fine pencil to trace the grasshopper design on page 153 on to the rice paper six times. Cut out the grasshoppers carefully using a fine pair of sharp scissors.

Attach the grasshoppers to the sides of the cake using some softened sugarpaste – take care not to get the paste too wet as this will cause the rice paper to dissolve.

4 Melt a small amount of cocoa butter on a saucer above a mug filled with just boiled water. Mix lavender, white and bluebell dusting powders into some of the cocoa butter. Using a fine paintbrush, begin to colour in the grasshopper cut-outs.

Outline the shape and add detail with green dusting powder mixed with cocoa butter. Add some detail dot work to the surface of the cake using green-coloured cocoa butter.

5 Cut out some small abstract, freehand blossom shapes, attach them to the cake and paint as for the grasshoppers. Paint a few small freehand leaves around each of the blossoms.

6 Finally, insert a celpick into the cake and then position the blue glory bower spray into it. Curve the stem over on to the front of the cake.

Blue Glory Bower
(Clerodendron ugandense)

There are about 400 different species of *Clerodendron*. This type is from tropical Africa, where it is known as the 'blue glory bower', or sometimes the 'blue butterfly bush', because of its butterfly-like flowers. The plant can grow up to 2.5 metres (8ft) tall and nearly 2 metres (6ft) across. It is a very useful flower for decorating men's cakes and for finishing wedding cakes that need a truly blue, decorative touch.

stamens

1 Cut the tips from one end of four white seed-head stamens and the tips from both ends of one extra stamen. Use the extra stamen as the pistil and then position the remaining four slightly below the tip of the pistil. Glue the base of the stamens together with a tiny amount of glue. Allow to firm a little and then glue to a 26-gauge white wire. Squeeze the stamens firmly on to the wire to secure them in place. Allow to dry. Dust the tips using a mixture of lavender, bluebell and deep purple dusting powders.

flowers

2 Knead a small amount of white flower paste until it is very pliable. Roll the paste into a ball and then a cone shape. Pinch the base of the cone,

materials

Small white seed-head stamens
Non-toxic high-tack craft glue
28-, 26- and 22-gauge white wire
Lavender, bluebell, deep purple, vine, forest green and foliage dusting powders (petal dust/blossom tint)
White, pale and mid-green, holly/ivy flower paste (gum paste)
Egg white
$\frac{1}{2}$ glaze
Nile green floristry tape

◆

equipment

Fine-nosed pliers and wire cutters
Grooved board
Harebell cutter [APR] or small blossom cutter [OPF9]
Simple leaf cutters [TT]
Plain edge cutting wheel [PME]
Sharp scalpel
Foam pad
Small celpick
Philadelphus leaf veiners [GI]

leaving a node to form the back of the flower. Place the paste against the board and roll out the area around the node.

3 Use the cutters to cut out the flower shape. (The flower pictured here has been cut out using a harebell

cutter. This is made in Zimbabwe and can be difficult to obtain, so see the address under 'Suppliers'.)

Place the flower on a pad and soften the edges of all five petals, stretching each to form an oval shape. All of the finished petals should have a slightly cupped shape, and one needs to be stretched a bit longer than the others.

4 Indent the centre of the flower using the pointed end of a small celpick. Moisten the base of the stamens with fresh egg white and thread the stamens through the centre of the flower. Pinch the back of the flower firmly to secure the shape.

Next, reposition each of the petals. The longest (the head) should be in front of the two arms, with the legs protruding behind the arms. Leave a large gap for the stamens, which should curl towards the long petal. Allow the

paste to dry and then attach a small ball of green paste to the base of each small flower.

buds

5 Bend a hook in the end of several short lengths of 28-gauge white wire. Attach a small ball of very pale green paste to the end of each length, rolling the base of each slightly to form a neck. Divide the tip into five using a sharp scalpel.

colouring

6 Dust the flowers and the tips of each bud with a mixture of bluebell and lavender dusting powders. Overdust the longest petal with deep purple dusting powder. (Take care when dusting these flowers as they are extremely fragile.) Dust the calyx and the base of

each of the buds with vine green powder. When complete, steam the flowers to set the colour.

leaves

7 Roll out some mid-green flower paste on to a grooved board. Cut out a leaf shape using one of the simple leaf cutters (you will need to make the leaves in pairs and graduate the sizes).

8 Insert a moistened 28- or 26-gauge white wire, depending upon the size of the leaf. Use a sharp scalpel to remove three or four slender cuts from both edges of the leaf. Soften the edges of the leaf and then vein using a philidelphus leaf veiner.

Repeat to make as many leaves as required. Dust the leaves with forest green, before overdusting with vine and foliage green. Dip into a ½ glaze.

assembly

9 Tape together small groups of buds and flowers using half width nile green floristry tape. The buds and flowers should work from one side to the other, down the stem. Make plenty of smaller sprays and then join together on to a main 22-gauge wire, adding two leaves at each junction. Dust the stem with the various green dusting powders.

Tree Frog Birthday Cake

This very grand, two-tiered cake was designed to be used at a large birthday celebration. I am very fond of tree frogs and could not complete this book without at least one! In the past, I have always modelled frog designs on to cakes using freehand techniques, but on this cake I decided to use a commercially available tree frog mould. The red silk cotton tree also provides a stunning feature on this cake, making it an eye-catching centrepiece.

cake & decoration

15cm (6in) and 25cm (10in) oval-shaped rich fruit cakes
Apricot glaze
1.5kg (3lb) white almond paste (marzipan)
Clear alcohol (kirsch, white rum, cointreau etc)
2kg (4lb) white sugarpaste (rolled fondant), coloured with sunny lime paste food colour
Small amount of royal icing
Green ribbon to trim the base of the cakes
Green velvet ribbon to trim the cake board
Non-toxic glue stick
Flower paste (gum paste) and sugarpaste mixed together in equal proportions
Vine, holly/ivy, black, lemon, red, primrose, cornflower blue and bridal satin dusting powders (petal dust/blossom tint)

◆

equipment

Sugarpaste smoothers
36cm (14in) oval cake board
Frog template (see p.153)
3 cake picks [W]
Tree frog mould [GI]
Firm, soft brush
Fine paintbrush

◆

flowers

7 red silk cotton tree flowers
11 sets of leaves (various sizes) and 5 buds (see p.46)

preparation

1 Brush the cakes with apricot glaze and cover with white almond paste. Allow to dry before brushing with clear alcohol, then cover with lime-coloured sugarpaste. Cover the cake board with sugarpaste and position the base tier on top. Use the smoothers to create a neat join between the board and the bottom edge of the cake. Off-set the top tier on top of the base tier.

board design

2 Trace and cut out the frog template shape on page 153. Put the template on top of the sugarpaste-coated board and use a firm but soft brush to dust around the edge with a mixture of vine green and holly/ivy dusting powders. Remove the template, reposition and repeat until the whole board is covered with frogs. Outline each of the designs with a fine brush and holly/ivy and vine green dusting powders mixed together with alcohol.

3 Attach a band of green ribbon to the base of each cake and trim the board with green velvet ribbon.

tree frog

4 Mix together equal amounts of sugarpaste and flower paste. Pack this paste into the frog mould. Trim off the excess and freeze for 20–30 minutes. Remove from the mould and allow to defrost and dry before colouring.

5 Dust the feet with a mixture of lemon and primrose and overdust with red dusting powder. Paint the body and legs with a mix of vine green and holly/ivy dusting powders. Paint the eye with red dusting powder and then add the pupil and outline with black dusting powder. Add some cornflower blue markings to the side of the body, allow to dry. Dust gently with bridal satin dusting powder to give it a gentle shine.

6 Wire up three branches of red silk cotton tree flowers and insert each stem into the display.

Festive Ideas

Candles are a popular feature throughout the year, but they are especially significant at Christmas. In fact, Christmas would not be complete in my house without flowers, chocolates and candles! In these arrangements, I have used the flower which I have most recently enjoyed teaching – the red silk cotton tree flower.

above: A single flower is used here to decorate a box of chocolates.
opposite: Red silk cotton tree flowers are used to maximum effect with a green spiral candle holder and matching textured candle.

Red Silk Cotton Tree Flower

(Bombax ceiba)

One of the eight species of *Bombax*, this flower is a native of India and the drier parts of Burma. When the fruit from the tree are fully ripe, they split to reveal a tangle of silky hairs and small black seeds. The silky material (like kapok) is used for stuffing cushions and other similar objects. The flowers of the tree are very large – I have scaled down the flowers and foliage a little to make them more suitable to decorate cakes. There is also a white version of *Bombax*, but the flowers are more open and the petal shape slightly thinner than the one featured here. I first saw this tree during a brief visit to Hong Kong and have been captivated by it ever since.

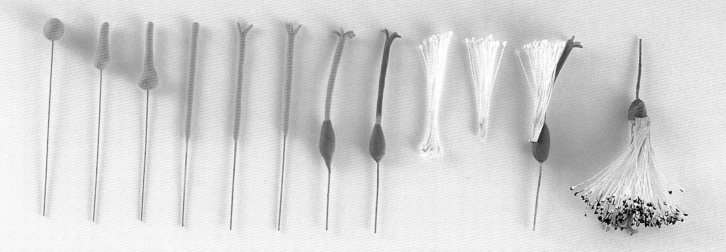

materials

Poppy and holly/ivy flower paste
(gum paste)
26-, 24-, 20- and 18-gauge white wire
Scarlet, burnt umber
and deep magenta craft dusts
White, pink, nile green and brown
floristry tape
White seed-head stamens
Non-toxic high-tack craft glue
Isopropyl alcohol
Primrose, lemon, vine green, aubergine,
forest, holly/ivy and nutkin brown/black
dusting powders (petal dust/
blossom tint)
½ glaze

◆

equipment

Fine scissors
Grooved board
Amaryllis cutter – side petal cutter only
[TT748]
Rose petal cutters [TT276–280]
Narrow Casablanca lily veiner [GI]
Large gardenia veiner [GI]
Dresden veining tool
Fine-nosed pliers
Wire cutters
Fine-angled tweezers

pistil

Roll a ball of pale poppy coloured paste and insert a 24-gauge white wire. Work the paste between your finger and thumb to cover a length of 5–7.5cm (2–3in). Smooth the length of the pistil between your palms and then give the whole thing a slight curve. Using a fine pair of scissors, cut the end of the pistil into five sections. Pinch each section between your finger and thumb, then curl them back. Dust with scarlet craft dust. Allow to dry. Attach a green oval-shaped ovary to the base of the pistil. Tape the pistil to an 18-gauge wire. Alternatively, you might prefer to make the pistil with floristry tape, which helps cut down on the number of breakages.

Twist a length of white or pink half width (or quarter width) floristry tape back on to itself to form a long, twisted strand. Cut the length into five sections and then tape them on to a piece of 24-gauge wire. Curl the tips and dust with scarlet craft dust.

stamens

2 You will need at least a full bunch of seed-head stamens per flower – quite often I end up using almost two bunches but this will depend on how large the bunches of stamens are. Divide the bunch into groups of 15–20 stamens. Using a small amount of non-toxic craft glue, attach the base of each group together. Allow to dry and then trim off the excess stamen from the glued end. The length of the stamen should be slightly shorter than the pistil.

3 Dilute a small amount of burnt umber craft dust with isopropyl alcohol and paint the tips of the stamens. (Some of the *Bombax* species have a mustard yellow tipped stamen.)

Allow to dry. Using a small amount of craft glue or some softened flower paste (with egg white), attach the stamens around the pistil. Allow to dry and then, using tweezers, curl the stamens back slightly. Gently dust the length of the filaments with some vine green dusting powder.

petals

4 Roll out some poppy-coloured paste, leaving a thick ridge down the centre – you may prefer to use a grooved board for this. Cut out the petal shapeusing the amaryllis cutter. Insert a moistened 26-gauge white wire into the petal, about half-way in. Soften the edges of the petal and then vein the surface with the narrow Casablanca lily veiner. Add extra creases in the petal with the broad end of the dresden tool. Pinch the tip of the petal and allow to semi-dry with a very slight curl. Repeat this process to make five petals.

5 Dust the petals at the base with a mixture of lemon and primrose dusting powders. Colour the edges and the majority of the petal with scarlet and deep magenta craft dust. Dust the very base and tip of each petal with vine green dusting powder.

6 Tape the petals around the stamens with full width nile green floristry tape. You may need to re-shape the petals a little in order to achieve the desired effect.

7 Attach a ball of poppy-coloured paste over the base of the petals to create a padded back to the flower. This will be covered with a calyx so do not worry if it is a bit untidy.

calyx

8 Roll out some holly/ivy flower paste and cut out three rose petal shapes. Place the shapes on a pad and soften the edges with the rounded end of a celstick. Cup the centre of each, paint with egg white and then attach over the back of the flower with the point of each sepal facing upwards. Pinch each tip into a sharp point. Dust with vine green dusting powder and then overdust with holly/ivy powder.

buds

9 Bend an open hook in the end of a 20-gauge wire. Form a ball of poppy-coloured flower paste into a cone. Shape and insert the moistened, hooked wire into the broad end. Using a cage, divide the bud into fine sections. Pinch each section between your finger and thumb to produce finer petals. Spiral the petals around the bud. Add a calyx using the same technique as that used for the flower, this time using a slightly smaller rose petal cutter.

leaves

10 Roll out some holly/ivy flower paste leaving a thick ridge to insert the wire. Using the plain edge cutting wheel, cut out a basic long leaf shape. Insert a moistened 26- or 24-gauge wire, depending on the size of the leaf. Work the base of the leaf firmly

between your finger and thumb to thin it out and produce a thicker stem.

11 Place the leaf on a pad and soften the edges. Vein using the large gardenia leaf veiner. Pinch the base and the tip firmly to accentuate the central vein and give the leaf some shape. Repeat to make five leaves for each set. the smaller the leaves, the narrower they should be.

colouring

12 Dust the edges of each leaf with aubergine dusting powder, overdust the whole leaf with forest green, vine green and holly/ivy dusting powder. Dip into a ½ glaze. Allow to dry and then tape together two sets of five leaves. Add a 22-gauge wire to the main stem to support the leaves.

assembly

13 Tape the flowers, buds and leaves on to 18-gauge wires using brown floristry tape. To thicken the bract, use shredded kitchen paper and tape over with brown tape. Everytime you add a bud or flower, tape in a set of leaves at the axil. To create a texture to the stem, twist some brown tape back on to itself to form a long strand. Wrap the strand at intervals, especially at the base of the buds and flowers. The flower and buds should appear directly from the main bract – I often use artistic license and give some of the flowers a short stem, just to add height to a spray for a cake.

14 Smooth the stem with the sides of a pair of scissors. Dust with nutkin brown or black dusting powder. Seal the colour on to the stem using some hi-tack craft glue. Allow to dry.

Eternal Flame

Flame lilies have been used to create ultimate impact on this stunning two-tiered wedding cake. I had originally planned to use a complicated combination of flowers and foliage as decoration, but in the end I decided to use only the lilies, as they can be very strong and dramatic when applied in such a simple way.

cake & decoration

20cm (8in) teardrop-shaped polystyrene dummy cake or rich fruit cake
30cm (12in) teardrop-shaped rich fruit cake
Apricot glaze
2kg (4lb) white almond paste (marzipan)
Clear alcohol (kirsch, white rum, cointreau etc)
1.5kg (3lb) white sugarpaste (rolled fondant) mixed with an equal amount of champagne sugarpaste
Small amount of royal icing
Fine gold ribbon to trim the base of the cakes
Broad gold ribbon to trim the edge of the cake board
Yellow, green and red dusting powders, together with three gold [SK] dusting powders (petal dust/blossom tint)
Non-toxic glue stick

◆

equipment

Sugarpaste smoothers
36cm (14in) oval cake board
Inexpensive sharp knife
Sharp scalpel or scriber
34cm (13in) curved candle holder
Gold spray paint
Fine and medium paintbrushes
Florists' pin holder
Celpick (optional)

◆

flowers

3 stems of flame lilies (see p.56)

preparation

1 Brush the large cake with apricot glaze and cover with almond paste. Leave to dry overnight. Moisten the surface with clear alcohol and then cover with sugarpaste, using smoothers to achieve a good finish. Apply firm, even pressure, with quick movement – do not stop suddenly, otherwise the two sugar surfaces will stick together.

2 Cover the cake board with sugarpaste and position the cake on top. Use the sugarpaste smoothers again to form a neat join around the base of the cake and the board. Allow to dry.

top tier

3 The top tier of this display could be a real cake, although I tend to use dummies for arrangements at great heights! To sculpt the polystyrene into the correct shape, heat an old knife until red hot. Taking care not to burn yourself, carefully cut away sections to form a rounded teardrop shape. (Bear in mind that the knife will be completely useless for any other task once it has been used to cut polystyrene.) Insert a florists' pin holder into the base of the shape to hold it in position. The pin will be hidden with the sugarpaste coating.

4 Brush the polystyrene with clear alcohol and cover with sugarpaste. Trim off the excess paste at the base (and possibly the back) and then form the excess paste at the tip into a finer point. Twist the tip slightly and allow to dry.

side design

5 Mix together the three gold dusting powders using some clear alcohol and a medium-sized paintbrush. Paint freehand leaf tendril designs on to both cakes. Highlight the shapes by etching the design with a sharp scalpel or scriber. Dust around the painted work with yellow, green and red dusting powders.

6 Attach a band of gold ribbon around the base of both cakes. Glue the gold ribbon to the edge of the cake board using a non-toxic glue stick.

assembly

7 Spray the curved candle holder with gold spray paint in a well-ventilated area and allow to dry. Position the top tier on the platform of the candle holder. Arrange the flame lilies around the cake.

If you have decided to use a fruit cake, you will need to insert the wires into a celpick and then into the cake. However, if you are using a polystyrene dummy, the wires can be inserted carefully into the shape (see step 3) and concealed with carefully positioned foliage.

Arrange two stems of flame lilies around the length of the candle holder – try to create a growing pattern. Next, position the base tier at the foot of the candle holder and then prop it up on an angled piece of wood to form an attractive tilt. Add a single flower at the base of the cake. Stand back from the display and then re-arrange as necessary.

Hothouse Flower

I spotted this strange container in my local florists some time ago but had managed to resist buying it until just a few days before one of my photoshoots; she was sitting on a shelf looking very tortured with a candle stuck in the top of her head! I have used flame lilies and red-feathered gerberas in a fairly simple way to create an ornamental display piece. After much discussion, she was eventually christened 'Hothouse flower' – a lucky escape from being called 'Hot head', though it might remain her nickname!

flowers

3 red-feathered gerberas (see p.59)
5 flame lilies, various sizes
3 half-open flame lilies (see p.56)
Several stems of flame lily foliage
with buds (see p.56)

◆

equipment

18-gauge wire
Florists' green staysoft or a small block
of dry oasis
Fine-nosed pliers
Wire cutters
Nile green floristry tape
Non-toxic high-tack craft glue
Decorative female head container or other
suitable container
Dried reindeer moss (optional)

preparation

1 First of all, you will need to strengthen and elongate any of the flower stems that need support and additional length. To do this, tape extra 18-gauge wire on to the existing flower stems.

Place a block of florists' staysoft next to a warm radiator in order to soften it slightly. (Otherwise, you may find it difficult to knead the material into the required shape.)

Put a large piece of the staysoft into the bottom of the vase, pressing it down firmly to ensure that it is secure and that there is an even distribution of weight. Alternatively, you may prefer to use dry oasis in the base; this will need to be cut into the correct shape using a sharp knife. Then, wedge the oasis firmly into the bottom of the vase.

assembly

2 Arrange the three red-feathered gerberas very close to the edge of the vase at the front, so that they frame the top of the head. One of the flowers should be fixed in a fairly central position.

3 Next, start to add the stems of flame lilies. Take care when arranging these around the spiky gerberas, as the flowers can become damaged. Try to ensure a variety of height in the arrangement and trail some of the flower stems and foliage down on to the sides of the face.

4 Finally, use the reindeer moss and a small amount of non-toxic glue to hide any excess staysoft that might be visible. Stand back from the arrangement and make any necessary adjustments.

Vibrant Table Arrangements

I love combining strong colours together in floral arrangements, and red and purple is one of my favourite pairings! Here, I have used flame lilies (page 56) and Brazilian violet trumpet vine (page 68). Remember to add plenty of strong, green foliage, which will help to marry the two colours together.

above: An effective table display can be created by using a few flowers to decorate each place setting.
opposite: This majestic red and purple arrangement could be used as a table centrepiece at a special anniversary dinner party.

Flame Lily
(Gloriosa rothschildiana, simplex and superba)

Flame lilies from tropical Africa and India have been cultivated in
Great Britain since 1902, although they are now mainly grown in
the Netherlands as a hothouse flower for the floristry trade.
The leaves terminate in a tendril, which the plant uses for
climbing. The flowers are available in a range of yellow and
red combinations, and the size and
petal shape of this family can
vary dramatically. Bear in
mind, however, that all
parts of this plant are
extremely poisonous!

materials

Pale melon, creamy lemon and mid-
holly/ivy flower paste (gum paste)
28-, 26-, 24-, 22- and 20-gauge
white wire
Deep magenta and scarlet craft dusts
Isopropyl alcohol
Primrose, lemon, moss, vine green,
forest and holly/ivy dusting powders
(petal dust/blossom tint)
Nile green floristry tape
¹/₂ glaze

◆

equipment

Flame lily template (see p.153)
Plain edge cutting wheel [PME]
Sharp scalpel
Foam pad
Celstick
Plain-edged angled tweezers
Medium-sized paintbrush
Fine-nosed pliers and wire cutters

petals

1 Roll out some pale melon flower paste, leaving a thick ridge down the centre. (You can use a grooved board if you prefer.) Place the petal template on top of the paste and cut out a petal using either a sharp scalpel or plain edge cutting wheel.

2 Insert a moistened 26-gauge wire into about half the length of the thick ridge of the petal, holding the paste firmly between your finger and thumb to prevent the wire from piercing through the paste. Put the petal on a pad and soften the edges using the rounded end of a celstick. The edges should be slightly wavy, but not too frilly as this will make the petal difficult to colour later.

3 Pinch the petal between your finger and thumb from the base to the tip. Using a pair of plain-edged angled tweezers, pinch a narrow triangular shape at the base of the petal. Curl the petal and allow to firm a little before colouring. Repeat to make six petals in total.

colouring

4 Dilute some scarlet and a touch of deep magenta craft dust with isopropyl alcohol. Then, using a medium-sized flat paintbrush loaded with some colour, paint a curved V-shape on to the upper surface of the petal. The design should taper at the sides to leave a border about half the length of the petal. Do the same on the back of the petal, taking the V-shape

from the base of the petal. Next, fill in the upper section and the back of the petal to give a concentrated red colour to the petal. Try to keep the brush strokes strong and do not use too much alcohol, as this will dilute the mixture. Repeat with the other five petals.

Allow the red to dry before dusting the base with a mixture of primrose and lemon dusting powders. Overdust the pinched triangular shape with a mixture of moss and vine green powders.

pistil and ovary

5 The pistil is made from nile green floristry tape. Twist a length of quarter width tape back on to itself to form a long strand. Cut to form three short lengths. Tape the three pieces to the end of a 26-gauge wire, again using quarter width tape. Curl the three ends back slightly.

At the base of the pistil there is an ovary that is divided into three sections. To make this section, roll a ball of green paste and attach it to the base of the pistil. Form the ball into an oval shape

and then divide it into three using a sharp scalpel, Pinch each section between your finger and thumb to form a slight ridge. Dust with vine green and moss dusting powders before coating with a 1/2 glaze.

stamens

6 Cut six lengths of 28-gauge wire. Use a pair of fine-nosed pliers to bend a flat hook in one end of each wire, then hold the hook halfway down its length and bend it again to form a T-bar shape. (Take care not to make this too large.)

The length (filament) of each stamen is quite fleshy and this can be re-created by simply taping over each wire several times with quarter width white floristry tape. However, a more effective finish can be achieved by applying a thin layer of paste to each stamen. Take a small sausage of white paste and wrap it around a dry wire. Work the paste against the wire, forcing some of the paste to the base of the T-bar shape. The tip of each stamen should be finer than the base, and the length should be

no longer than the length of a petal. Smooth the length of each filament and then carefully bend them into a curve.

7 Attach a small sausage of white paste over the T-bar to form the anther. Divide the upper length of each anther in half using a sharp scalpel.

8 Dust the anthers with a mixture of primrose and lemon dusting powders, and the filaments with vine green fading slightly towards the base of the anther. (Although a touch of red can also appear on the anthers, I tend to avoid using this, as it can look like a mistake.)

9 Tape the six stamens evenly around the base of the pistil using half width nile green floristry tape. If the stamens are too long at this stage, simply pinch off the excess before taping each into place. The flower paste should still be slightly wet, so you can re-shape the stamens if necessary.

assembly

10 Tape a 20-gauge wire on to the stamens using half width nile green tape. Next, tape the petals around the stamens, attaching one petal to each stamen. Pull the petals back slightly and then bend the main stem with the pliers. Re-shape the petals if required.

buds

11 Bend an open hook in the end of a half length 24-gauge wire. Form a sharp, pointed cone of pale melon flower paste and insert the moistened hooked wire into the base. Pinch the paste on to the wire to secure it in place. Divide the surface of the bud into three sections and then pinch a ridge down each section using the tweezers. Then, carefully twist the tip of the bud slightly.

leaves

12 Roll out some mid-green flower paste, leaving a thick ridge along

the centre to insert the wire. Using the cutting wheel, cut out a freehand leaf shape, making sure that it tapers into a fine point. (I do not make them to the correct size as the leaves would be too vulnerable and liable to break.) Insert a moistened 26-, 24- or 22-gauge wire into the leaf (depending upon your chosen size).

13 Vein the surface of the leaf gently with the cutting wheel, taking care not to cut through the paste. Use the same wheel to create a central vein along the leaf, this time using a little more pressure. Use your finger and thumb to pinch along the leaf from the base to the tip.

   Repeat this process to make a number of leaves in various sizes.

14 It is important to dust the leaves before they have dried, as this will help to avoid damage to the fine tips. Use moss, vine green and holly/ivy powders, curl the tips of each leaf and then allow to dry. Finally, dip the leaves iinto a ½ glaze.

note

The half-open flowers are made in the same manner as the fully open flowers, but are smaller and coloured with less red powder. The petals should all form a point at the tip.

Red-feathered Gerbera

These wonderful flowers are very intricate – each petal is partially split into three sections. Although they are time-consuming and extremely fragile, they are great fun to make! This type of gerbera can be found in various sizes and colours, including white, pink, apricot, orange, red and yellow.

---

materials

Deep pink and green flower paste (gum paste)
30- and 18-gauge wire
Scarlet and deep magenta craft dusts
Isopropyl alcohol
Egg white
Mimosa sugartex
Aubergine, forest and holly/ivy dusting powders (petal dust/blossom tint)

◆

equipment

Cymbidium orchid sepal cutters [TT23]
Fine scissors
Small ball tool
Flat paintbrush
Dresden veining tool
Celstick

---

petals

1 Roll out a piece of pink paste, leaving a thick strip at the base. Cut out several petals with the orchid cutter. Insert a moistened 30-gauge white wire.

2 Use scissors to divide each petal into three, removing slender V-shaped pieces. Use the small ball tool to soften the edges and then vein down the centre of each section with the fine end of the veining tool. Pinch the tips and carefully stretch each section. Repeat to make 38–50 petals. Apply scarlet and deep magenta craft dusts mixed with alcohol but do not dilute too much – otherwise the colour will be streaky.

stamens

3 Bend a large open hook in the end of a length of 18-gauge wire. Moisten and attach a ball of pink paste. Flatten the top and then snip the surface, forming tiny, hair-like petals. Indent the centre slightly with the rounded end of a celstick. Dust with aubergine dusting powder.

4 Roll a length of green paste and cut a rectangular shape. Make cuts along one side of the strip to suggest a comb. Soften the edges with the dresden tool. Cut off the tips of several stamens and cut the lengths into short strands. Moisten each strand with egg white and attach them at intervals along the strip. Moisten the dried centre and wrap the length of paste around the it. Repeat 3–4 times before painting and dusting the paste in the same way as the petals. Moisten the tips of the stamens and dip into mimosa sugartex to create pollen-tipped stamens. Tape the petals around the centre of the stamen – leave some wire showing at the base, as this will be covered by the calyx.

calyx

5 Shape a ball of green paste into a cone and hollow out the centre using the celstick. Attach to the back of the gerbera. Roll numerous, pointed strands of paste, then flatten, vein and attach over the base shape. Dust with forest and holly/ivy powders. Add a ring of aubergine between the base of the petals and the tips of the sepals.

Pink and Lilac Engagement Cake

This pretty cake was originally designed for an engagement celebration but it could just as easily be used for a small wedding reception, or it could even serve as an 18th or 21st birthday cake. It has been turned into an impressive centrepiece – I added extra height to the display by placing a tall candle holder with a candle positioned behind the cake. However, do be careful not to allow the candle flame to burn too close to the sugar, otherwise the results could be disastrous!

cake & decoration

25cm (10in) teardrop-shaped rich fruit cake
Apricot glaze
1.25kg (2½lb) white almond paste
(marzipan)
Clear alcohol (kirsch, white rum,
cointreau etc)
2kg (4lb) white sugarpaste (rolled fondant)
African violet, lavender, white and deep
purple dusting powders
(petal dust/blossom tint)
Light silver metallic lustre dust [SK]
Small amount of royal icing or
softened sugarpaste
Fine lilac ribbon to trim the cake base
Soft lilac ribbon to trim the cake board
Non-toxic glue stick

◆

equipment

Sugarpaste smoothers
36cm (14in) oval cake board
Scroll stencil [TSL]
30-gauge silver reel wire
26cm (10¼in) silver-finish candle holder
14cm (5½in) lilac candle
Fine-nosed pliers
Wire cutters
Cake pick (optional)

◆

flowers

2 Pink and Lilac Engagement Sprays
(see p.62)

preparation

1 Brush the cake with warmed apricot glaze and cover with white almond paste. Allow to dry – overnight if possible. Moisten the surface of the almond paste with clear alcohol and cover with white sugarpaste. Use a pair of sugarpaste smoothers to achieve a good finish. (A ball of softened sugarpaste, pressed into the palm of your hand, is useful for smoothing the edges and tight curves but always use a fast, smoothing action to prevent the sugarpaste from sticking.)

2 Cover the cake board with sugarpaste and position the cake on top. Use the smoothers to ease the paste from the cake on to the board and to create a neat join.

stencil design

3 The stencil design used here is simply a small detail from a long piece of scroll work. In order to get the design close to the base of the cake, you may need to cut up the stencil into several parts. Use a mixture of silver lustre dust and lavender, African violet and deep purple dusting powders to dust the design on to the board and also the surface of the cake. Overdust the design and the surface of the cake gently using only the light silver lustre dust.

assembly

4 Use royal icing or softened sugarpaste to attach a band of fine lilac ribbon around the base of the cake. (The consistency of diluted sugarpaste should be similar to that of royal icing.) Next, secure a band of ribbon around the board edge using the non-toxic glue.

5 Wire up two pink and lilac engagement sprays as instructed on page 62. Use the fine silver reel wire to secure the smaller spray to the side of the candle holder. Insert the candle into the holder and then position behind the cake. The larger spray simply rests on top of the cake but, alternatively, it can be inserted into a cake pick and then into the cake itself.

Pink and Lilac Engagement Spray

Vines are ideal material to use as inspiration and as a starting point for many types of arrangements and sprays. Because of their trailing nature, they make elegant partners to many other flowers; here the Brazilian trumpet vine makes a wonderful partner to the Brazilian kapok tree flowers.

flowers

3 trailing stems of Brazilian violet
trumpet vines (see p.68)
2 Brazilian kapok tree flowers,
plus 5 buds and 2 sets of leaves (see p.64)
2 stems of tuberoses (see p.67)

◆

equipment

18-gauge wire
Wire cutters
Fine-nosed pliers
Nile green floristry tape

preparation

I Tape together three trailing stems of trumpet vine, using 18-gauge wire for each of the main stems. Wire together one spray longer than the others.

assembly

2 Tape the longest stem of trumpet vine on to the half-open kapok flower using half width nile green floristry tape. Add the group of five buds and tape in securely. Then add the fully opened kapok flower as the focal point.

3 Tape in the other two stems of trumpet vine. Add the two stems of tuberose, positioning them opposite one another to run a line through the spray. Complete the shape by adding the Brazilian kapok leaves to both sides of the spray. Cut off any excess wire and tape over the handle of the spray with full width floristry tape to neaten. Attach to the candle holder as explained on page 60 and position.

Brazilian Kapok Tree Flower

(Chorisia speciosa)

Chorisia is part of the same family as the *bombax* (see page 46). This large tree produces spectacular crimson, pink or white five-petalled flowers before the leaves start to appear on the tree; it is only towards the end of the flowering season that both are seen together. The trunk of the tree is heavily studded with thorns that disappear as the tree ages. As the name implies, this tree produces a kapok-type floss that surrounds the seeds.

materials

30-, 26-, 24-, 22- and 18-gauge white wire
White and mid-holly/ivy flower paste
(gum paste)
White, nile green and beige
floristry tapes
Primrose, lemon, plum, white, forest
green, aubergine, vine, foliage green,
brown and nutkin brown dusting
powders (petal dust/blossom tint)
Cyclamen liquid food colour
$1/2$ glaze
Kitchen paper
Non-toxic high-tack craft glue

equipment

Fine-angled pliers
Grooved board
Sharp scalpel
Large rose petal cutter [TT550]
or template (see p.153)
Small rose petal cutter [TT279]
Very large rose petal veiner [GI]
Fine paintbrush
Celstick
Plain edge cutting wheel [PME]
Homalomena leaf veiner
or similar [GI]
Foam pad

stamens

1 There are five fleshy curved stamens at the end of the long central platform. These can be modelled directly on to the centre, or they can be wired individually. To do this, bend a tiny hook in the end of five short lengths of 30-gauge wire. Attach a sausage of white paste to the end of each to form the anthers. Curve each of the anthers and then pinch the entire lengths with a pair of fine-angled pliers or a sharp scalpel.

2 Tape the five stamens together using quarter width white floristry tape. Squeeze the stamens together to make a nice, tight group. Allow to dry.

Roll a ball of white paste into a sausage and wrap this around the taped wire. Work the paste quickly between your finger and thumb to cover the length of wire, gently curving the length of the platform as you go.

At the centre of the stamens there is often a pistil protruding above the tips of the anthers – this is only visible in the mature flowers. If you wish to replicate this, cover a very short piece of 30-gauge wire with a sliver of white flower paste. This should then be taped into the set of stamens.

3 Dust the length of the platform with a mixture of white and plum dusting powders, fading the colour towards the base of the stamens. Dust the anthers with a mixture of white, primrose and lemon dusting powders.

petals

4 Roll out some white flower paste on to a grooved board, or roll out the paste with a small rolling pin, leaving the centre slightly thicker. Cut out the petal shape using either the template and a sharp scalpel or a rose petal cutter squashed into the shape of the template on page 153. Insert a moistened 26-gauge white wire into the thick ridge.

5 Put the petal in a large rose petal veiner. Press the two sides firmly to give full veining. Place the petal on a pad and gently soften the edges to give a slightly wavy edge. Repeat to make five petals. Allow to dry slightly with a gentle curve before dusting.

colouring & assembly

6 Dust each petal along the edges using a mixture of plum and white dusting powders. Apply a heavier pink along about one third of the curve, from the tip of each petal. Dust a patch of white on the remaining two thirds, and overdust with a primrose and lemon streak – this colouring should be quite pale. Finally, add a patch of aubergine dusting powder at the very base of each petal.

7 Use a fine paintbrush and cyclamen liquid colour to paint several short, tapered lines on to each petal as illustrated. Tape the five petals around the base of the stamen platform using half width nile green floristry tape. Ideally, the petals should still be a little damp at this stage, as this will enable you to manipulate the paste into a relaxed flower shape more easily.

calyx

8 Roll out some pale green paste quite thickly. Use the cutter, or a scalpel and template to cut out two rose petal shapes. Soften the edges of both sepals and then hollow out the centre with the rounded end of a large celstick. Moisten the base of both sepals and attach them at the base of the flower, overlapping the pair slightly.

Dust the paste with vine and foliage green dusting powders. Once dry, steam the flower to set the colour and leave a slight shine.

buds

9 Bend a hook in the end of a 24- or 22-gauge wire. Roll a ball of mid-holly/ivy paste and insert the moistened hooked wire into one end. Work the base of the bud down on to the wire, so that it forms a balloon shape. Then divide the bud in half using a sharp scalpel blade. Dust with forest green.

leaves

10 The leaves are rather like those of the red silk cotton tree flower (bombax) on page 46. The leaves can be in sets of five or seven and I have chosen a small group. Roll out some mid-green paste, leaving a thick ridge down the centre of the leaf. Cut out a basic leaf shape (see leaf design on page 153) using a plain edge cutting wheel. The lengths should graduate in a similar way to that of a

and overdust with foliage green and a little vine green. Allow to dry and dip into a ½ glaze. Tape the leaves into sets of five or seven using half width nile green tape.

assembly

13 Fix a group of buds on to the end of three taped 18-gauge wires using beige floristry tape. Where the buds join the main branch, I tend

process until you have created the required length/effect. Rub the taped branch with the side of a pair of scissors – this will smooth out the stem and leave a shine.

14 Dust the branch with nutkin brown and brown dusting powders. Seal with a thin layer of non-toxic high-tack craft glue to prevent the colour from running on to the surface of the cake.

hand, with the longest section in the centre, and two shorter pieces on either side.

11 Insert a moistened 24-gauge white wire into at least half the length of the thick ridge. The edges of the leaves are slightly serrated so use a sharp scalpel to cut into the edge of the leaf and then flick the paste to remove a sliver. Repeat at intervals around the leaf but do not make the cuts too deep. Soften the edges of each leaf and then vein the paste with the homalomena veiner (or something similar). Pinch the leaf from the base to the tip to accentuate the central vein.

12 Dust the edges of each leaf with aubergine dusting powder. Use forest green at the centre of the leaf

to add some twisted half width beige tape to form a ridged effect. This can produce a very obvious finish to the branch – if you prefer something more subtle, try taping over the top of the ridged tape. Thicken the branch as you work down the length by using some shredded kitchen paper underneath the tape. Continue to add bud groups before positioning a set of smaller leaves at the junction, again with some twisted tape. Add a flower with a set of leaves and more twisted tape. Continue this

Tuberose
(Polianthes tuberosa)

This is a very useful flower that complements many of the larger species that feature in this book. The plant originates from Mexico and has been used in the perfume industry in France for centuries.

materials

Small seed-head stamens
26-, 24- and 18-gauge white wire
Non-toxic high-tack craft glue
Lemon, primrose, vine green, plum,
white and holly/ivy dusting powders
(petal dust/blossom tint)
White flower paste (gum paste)
Egg white
Nile green floristry tape

◆

equipment

Six-petalled pointed blossom cutters
[OP N1, 2, 3]
Sharp scalpel
Dresden veining tool
Celstick
Fine-nosed pliers and wire cutters

stamens

1 Bend three seed-head stamens in half to form six. Trim the base and glue to the end of a 24-gauge wire. Dust the tips with lemon and primrose powders.

first & second layers

2 Roll out a small piece of paste, leaving a slightly thicker pimple at the centre. Cut out the smallest flower shape. Soften the edges and hollow out the length of each petal. Vein each petal three times using the fine end of the dresden tool.

3 Moisten the centre with fresh egg white and thread the stamens through the centre. Pinch the back of the flower shape to close up the petals around the stamens and allow to dry.
  Repeat the process, this time using the slightly larger cutter. Try to position each petal over a join in the previous layer. Allow to dry.

third layer

4 Roll a ball of paste into a long cone shape and pinch out the broad end to form a pedestal shape. Thin out the base with the celstick, but remember that tuberoses do have fleshy petals.
  Cut out the flower shape using the largest of the cutters. Soften the edges and hollow out the back of each petal. Vein as before. Open up the centre using the pointed end of the celstick.

5 Thread the dried centre through the back of the flower, again positioning a petal over a join. Thin the back if required and remove any excess paste. Divide the back into six sections using the sharp scalpel. Give the back a graceful curve.

buds

6 Insert a moistened 26-gauge wire into the base of a cone-shaped piece of white paste. Work the base of the cone down on to the wire to form a slender back. Divide the bud into three sections with the sharp scalpel

and pinch each section to create a subtle ridge. Vein the three sections slightly with the scalpel. Repeat to make buds of various sizes, bearing in mind that the the buds grow in pairs of approximately the same size.

assembly

7 Tape the buds in pairs, on to an 18-gauge wire using half width floristry tape. There should be a single bract at the base of each pair of buds – cut pointed bract shapes from full width nile green floristry tape, vein slightly and then tape into position. Add the flowers in pairs, together with single bracts.

8 Use vine green dusting powder on the buds, (the larger the buds, the paler the green). Tinge the buds and flowers with a mix of plum and white. Dust the bracts with vine green. and holly/ivy dusting powders.

Brazilian Violet Trumpet Vine

Despite its name, the flowers of this vine are quite pinkish in colour. I have also used some artistic licence by reducing the size of the blooms slightly and adding more blue to the violet colour, so that it blends well with the other flowers used on the Pink and Lilac Engagement Cake on page 62.

materials

Small seed-head stamens
26-, 24- and 18-gauge wire
Non-toxic high-tack craft glue
Primrose, white, plum, lavender, bluebell, deep purple, African violet, vine green, forest green and holly/ivy dusting powders (petal dust/blossom tint)
White and mid-holly/ivy flower paste (gum paste)
Egg white
Isopropyl alcohol
½ glaze
Nile green floristry tape

equipment

Celstick
Blossom cutter [TT475]
Fine scissors
Sharp scalpel
Ceramic silk veining tool
Fine-angled tweezers
Dresden veining tool
Small calyx cutters [OPR13, R13a]
Simple leaf cutters [TT225–232]
Large briar rose veiner [GI]
Fine-nosed pliers
Wire cutters
Fine paintbrush

stamens

1 Bend five stamens in half and glue them together. Once firm, trim off most of the length and glue to the end of a 24-gauge wire. Allow to dry before dusting the tips with primrose powder.

flower

2 Roll a ball of well-kneaded flower paste into a cone. Pinch out the broad end to form a pedestal. Use a celstick to roll out the paste on a board, creating a neat waistline at the base of the centre. Cut out the flower using the blossom cutter; you will need to offset the shape so that three of the petals are slightly longer.

3 Use the scissors to remove a fine sliver of paste from between each of the petals. Open up the throat with the pointed end of the celstick. Vein and frill each of the petals with the ceramic silk veining tool.

4 Use a pair of fine-angled tweezers to pinch a couple of ridges on the central base petal. Moisten the base of the stamens with egg white and pull them through the throat of the flower. Pinch the base of the flower and remove any excess length. Gently pinch the back of the flower to make it flat. Allow the base petals to firm up flat, and the two smaller petals to pull back slightly.

colouring

5 Dust the flower with a mixture of white, lavender and plum, or bluebell mixed with one of the purples.

Overdust across the veins on each petal with a stronger version of your chosen colour. Dust the back of the flower and the throat with vine green. Paint some fine veins on the flower with a dark mix of the colours and alcohol.

buds

6 Hook and moisten the end of a 26- or 24-gauge wire. Roll a ball of white paste into a cone and insert the hooked wire into the fine end. Divide the tip into five sections with the scalpel. Repeat to make buds of various sizes, including small buds in green paste.

calyx

7 Roll out some green paste quite finely and cut out a calyx shape for each flower and white bud. Soften the edges and then vein each sepal with the

fine end of the dresden tool. Pinch the tips and attach to the back of each flower and bud. Dust the calyx with holly/ivy and vine green dusting powders. Colour the buds as for the flowers.

leaves

8 Roll out some holly/ivy flower paste on to a grooved board and cut out the leaves, using one size of cutter for each set. Soften the edges of each leaf and vein with the briar rose leaf veiner. Pinch the leaf from the base to the tip to accentuate the central vein. Repeat to make leaves in various sizes.

9 Dust the edges of each leaf with African violet and then overdust with vine green, forest green and holly/ivy powders. Dry and dip into a ½ glaze. Cover the leaf stems with half width nile green tape and then tape into sets.

tendrils

10 Twist some quarter width nile green floristry tape into a fine strand. Cut three short lengths and then tape them to the end of a 26-gauge wire, leaving the central tendril longer than the other two. Twist the tendrils gently around a paintbrush handle.

assembly

11 Tape a set of tendrils to the end of an 18-gauge wire. Add a set of leaves. Continue down the stem adding groups of flowers and buds; each with two sets of leaves. Add the occasional tendril as you work along. Dust the main stem with the various green powders.

Red-feathered Gerbera Cake

Red and pink work extremely well together on this birthday cake, which features a single
red-feathered gerbera, pink South Sea Island ti leaves, eucalyptus and a red ink plant.
This helps to create a very richly coloured design with an exotic feel that is remarkably stylish.
Here, the flowers are positioned on a relatively small cake, but they would also
look good on something larger.

cake & decoration

30-, 28- and 26-gauge wires
17.5cm (7in) trefoil-shaped rich fruit cake
Apricot glaze
500g (1lb) white almond paste (marzipan)
Clear alcohol (kirsch, white rum,
cointreau etc)
750g (1½lb) pink sugarpaste
(rolled fondant)
Small amount of royal icing
Magenta organza-type ribbon to trim
the base of the cake
Red velvet ribbon to trim the edge of
the cake board
Non-toxic glue stick

◆

equipment

Sugarpaste smoothers
23cm (9in) round cake board
28cm (11in) pewter plate
Fine-nosed pliers
Wire cutters
Posy pick

◆

flowers

1 red-feathered gerbera (see p.59)
15 magenta South Sea Island ti leaves
(see p.26)
5 stems of red ink plant (see right)
5 stems of eucalyptus (see p.72)

preparation

Brush the cake with apricot glaze and
then cover with white almond paste.
Allow to dry overnight if possible.
  Moisten the surface of the almond
paste with clear alcohol and cover with
pale pink sugarpaste. Use a pair of
sugarpaste smoothers and a small
amount of softened sugarpaste to create
a smooth finish. Cover the cake board
with paste and position the cake on top.
Use the smoother to work the paste at
the base of the cake, helping to form a
neat, continuous join between the two.

2 Attach a band of magenta ribbon to
the base of the cake using a small
amount of royal icing. Tie three small
knotted bows and attach these to each
of the indents. Glue a length of red
velvet ribbon to the edge of the board
using the non-toxic glue stick.

3 Wire together a spray for the top
of the cake, taking care not to
damage the delicate gerbera petals.
Wire a smaller spray using the red ink
plant as a focal point.
  Insert the larger spray into a posy
pick and then into the cake. The smaller
spray simply rests at the base of the
cake. I have finished the design by
presenting the cake on a pewter plate.

red ink plant

This wonderful climbing herb produces
attractive berries from late summer to
autumn. It is remarkably simple to make
(see the instructions on page 26 in my
book *Floral Wedding Cakes & Sprays*)
and is the perfect complement to
the gerbera spray on this cake.

California Dreaming

A single matilija tree poppy flower forms the focal point of this very calm and soothing centrepiece. As the poppy blooms in both California and Mexico, I have teamed it with some Mexican tuberose stems and large eucalyptus leaves, which help to maintain the theme and set off the main flower. This cake makes a wonderful centrepiece for a silver or pearl wedding anniversary, but the arrangement would also make an unusual feature on a wedding or engagement cake.

cake & decoration

25cm (10in) elliptical-shaped (teardrop) rich fruit cake
Apricot glaze
1.25kg (2½lb) white almond paste (marzipan)
Clear alcohol (kirsch, white rum, cointreau etc)
2kg (4lb) white sugarpaste (rolled fondant)
Fine and broad soft blue/green ribbon to trim the cake and the board
Broad white sheer-textured ribbon to trim the edge of the cake
Non-toxic glue stick

◆

equipment

Sugarpaste smoothers
30cm (12in) round cake board
Florists' green staysoft or a small block of dry oasis
Small oval acrylic base [HP]

◆

flowers

1 matilija poppy, plus one bud and foliage (see p.74)
5 stems of tuberoses (see p.67)
5 stems of eucalyptus (see right)

preparation

1 Brush the cake with apricot glaze and cover with almond paste. Allow to dry. Moisten the surface of the almond paste with clear alcohol and cover with white sugarpaste, using sugarpaste smoothers to create a good finish. Cover the board with paste and transfer the cake on top of it. Leave everything aside to dry — preferably overnight.

2 Attach a band of broad blue/green ribbon to the base of the cake, followed by the broader, white sheer ribbon on top. Add a length of fine blue/green ribbon to this. Glue a length of ribbon to the edge of the board.

3 Glue a piece of staysoft to the acrylic base and allow to dry. Position the base into the indent of the teardrop cake and then carefully arrange the flowers in the staysoft. Start with the poppy flower and bud stems, and then add the tuberoses and eucalyptus.

eucalyptus

Eucalyptus is an ideal foliage for complementing many of the flowers used in this book. To make it, simply roll out some pale green flower paste and cut out the shape with a circle cutter. Insert a piece of 26- or 28-gauge wire into the central ridge and then soften the edges of the paste with a celstick. Vein the surface with a real leaf and allow to firm up with a slight curve (for an attractive finish).

Use dark green dusting powder to colour the leaf, before overdusting with holly/ivy and a little white. Tape a few strands of half width floristry tape to a 20-gauge wire, and add the small leaves in pairs. As you work down the stem, gradually position the larger leaves and add smaller stems for greater variety. Dust the main stem with dark green, aubergine and plum powders.

Matilija Poppy
(Romneya coulteri)

There are two species of *Romneya*, both found only in California and north-western Mexico.
The plant is a summer-flowering perennial that grows to over a metre (3ft) high, and produces single, large
white flowers with very crumpled petals, a mass of golden yellow stamens and striking blue-grey/green
foliage. *Romneyas* are wonderful, eye-catching flowers to use on summer wedding cakes as they are both
simple to make and yet at the same time delicate in appearance.

materials

28-, 26- and 20-gauge wire
Fine white lace-makers' cotton
thread [Brock 120]
Nile green floristry tape
Lemon, primrose, vine green,
holly/ivy, forest green and white dusting
powders (petal dust/blossom tint)
Cyclamen liquid food colouring [SK]
White and pale holly/ivy flower paste
(gum paste)
Egg white
¼ glaze

◆

equipment

Fine-nosed pliers
Wire cutters
Fine sharp scissors
Emery board
Broad flat paintbrush
Sharp scalpel
Petal templates (see p.154)
or large poppy cutters [TT513, 514]
Orchid veiner no.18 [CC]
Leaf templates (see p.154) or
chrysanthemum leaf cutters [HH]
Philodendron leaf or chrysanthemum
leaf veiner [GI]
Ceramic silk veining tool [HP]
Fine-angled tweezers
Foam pad
Cocktail stick (toothpick)

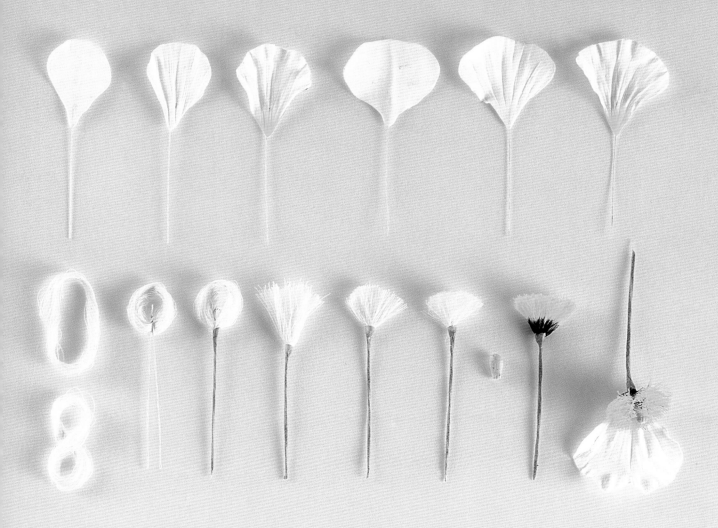

stamens

1 Bend a length of 26-gauge wire in half, and then twist the wire just below the bend using fine-nosed pliers to create a small loop. (The loop is used to hold the paste ovary at a later stage.)

2 Wrap the fine white thread around two parted fingers about 80 times. Remove the thread and twist the loop into a figure of eight. Bend the shape in half to form a smaller loop.

3 Place the looped wire through the centre of the thread and close the two lengths of the wire together to hold the thread firmly. Tape over the base of the thread and continue down the wire. Cut the thread loop open and then trim the stamens into a curved shape using your thumb nail as a guide line.

4 Rub the tips of the thread against an emery board to create fuzzy tips and to provide more bulk. Dust the stamens with a mixture of lemon and primrose dusting powders.

The heart of the stamen centre is a very dark burgundy colour – to achieve this, use a broad, flat paintbrush to apply a circle of cyclamen liquid colour to both the inside and outside of the stamen centre. Allow to dry.

ovary

5 Roll a ball of pale green paste and then form it into a cone shape. Flatten the narrow end and divide the surface into eight sections using a sharp scalpel. Texture the sides of the cone shape with the scalpel to create the impression of tiny hairs. Moisten the

hook at the centre of the stamens and position the paste ovary on top. Dust very lightly with vine green powder.

petals

6 Roll out some pure white flower paste quite thinly, leaving a thick ridge to insert a wire into the petal. Place one of the two sizes of petal template on top of the paste and cut out a petal using a sharp scalpel. Alternatively, use one of the poppy cutters although this will result in a slightly different shape. Remove the petal from the board and insert a hooked, moistened 26-gauge wire into the ridge.

7 Put the petal on the orchid veiner and press the petal firmly with the side of your hand. Remove the petal,

turn it over and repeat. Continue with this action until you have created a creased petal design.

Place the petal back on the board and use the ceramic silk veining tool to frill the upper curved edge of the petal. If you wish to make the other edges of the petal very fine, overfrill them with a cocktail stick. Pinch the base of the petal and cup slightly. Allow the shape to firm up a little, but not dry completely.

Repeat this process to make four large petals and then again for two smaller petals. Bear in mind that the smaller, finer petals will be very fragile, so take care not to overfrill.

colouring & assembly

8 Generally speaking, it is easier to dust the petals and wire the flower together before they have had a chance to dry thoroughly. To do this, dust a patch of vine green dusting powder on the base of each petal, on both the back and front. Tape the stamen centre on to a 20-gauge wire using half width nile green floristry tape.

Next, tape the two small petals tightly at the base of the stamens. Add the larger petals behind the small ones, to create a full flower shape. The petals should still be soft at this stage and you may be able to re-shape the flower to produce a pleasing finish.

Thicken the stem slightly using several layers of floristry tape, to add further strength.

leaves

9 Roll out some holly/ivy-coloured flower paste, leaving a thick ridge at the centre of the leaf. Use one of the leaf templates and a sharp scalpel to cut

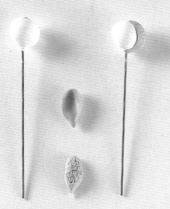

out the leaf. Insert a moistened 28- or 26-gauge white wire into the thick ridge. Place the leaf on a pad and soften the edges. Vein the leaf with the small philodendron veiner, using the back of the leaf to create raised veins on the front of the poppy leaf. Remove the leaf from the veiner and pinch from the base to the tip to give the leaf some

shape. Repeat this process to make plenty of leaves for the spray, ranging from small to large.

If you would prefer not to use templates for making so many leaves, try cutting a basic leaf shape with some chrysanthemum leaf cutters. Use a sharp scalpel to remove two V-shaped cuts from the middle section of each leaf, which will help to create a tri-lobed effect. Although this is not the exact shape, it will look effective when the poppy stems are taped together.

10 Dust the leaves with a touch of forest green and overdust with holly/ivy and white dusting powders. Steam the leaves to set the colour or dip them into a ¼ glaze.

buds

11 Bend a hook in the end of a 20-gauge wire. Roll a ball of white flower paste, moisten the hooked wire and insert it into the base. Divide the bud into three sections using a sharp scalpel blade. Create some fine veins, again using the blade in between each of the divisions.

12 To create the bracts on the bud, roll three, even-sized balls of green paste. Form each into a teardrop shape, flatten slightly between your finger and thumb and position on a pad. Hollow out each shape to thin and broaden the bract shapes. Moisten each bract with egg white and attach to the semi-dried bud.

Texture the surface of each bract with a pair of sharp scissors to create tiny hairs. (It is easier to do this with the wire held from above so that the bud is upside down.) Dust the bud in the same way as the leaves. Allow to dry.

13 Tape the leaves on to each flower and bud stem using half width nile green floristry tape. Begin with the smallest leaves, working around and down the stem, before reaching the larger leaves. Bend the stems slightly to give character to the plant.

Single Peony

materials

30-, 28-, 26-, 24- and 18-gauge
white wire
Pale melon and mid-holly/ivy flower
paste (gum paste)
Nile green floristry tape
Vine green, primrose, lemon, forest
green, aubergine, scarlet and holly/ivy
dusting powders
(petal dust/blossom tint)
Non-toxic high-tack craft glue
Scarlet craft dust
Pale lemon hammer-head stamens
$^1/_2$ glaze

◆

equipment

Fine-angled tweezers
Large and medium rose petal cutters
[TT549, 550, 551] or templates
(see p.155)
Small rose petal cutters
[TT276, 278, 279, 280] or templates
(see p.155)
Peony leaf cutters
Ceramic silk veining tool [HP]
Single peony leaf veiner [GI]
Nile green floristry tape
Fine-nosed pliers and wire cutters
Grooved board

Peonies (*Paeonia*) originate from China where they have been in cultivation for over 1000 years. The Chinese have used this plant for many medicinal purposes, one of which was as a cure for madness! I have made a huge number of these flowers over the last few years and it has not helped me at all – perhaps another few years and I will be cured! The colour selection is vast and ranges from white, cream, yellow and pink, to red, peach, magenta and burgundy.

ovary

Cut three short lengths of 26-gauge wire and bend a hook in the end of each. Roll a ball of green paste into a long teardrop shape and insert a moistened wire into the broad end. Pinch a ridge down the length of the teardrop and curl the tip of the shape over on to the ridge.

Repeat this process to make three sections. Tape the three sections together using half width nile green tape (this is best carried out before the paste has dried in order to get a tight centre). Dust the paste with vine green and catch each of the tips with a combination of aubergine and scarlet dusting powders. Tape on to an 18-gauge wire and then allow to dry.

stamens

2 Form six groups of stamens and glue each together using a small amount of glue. Squeeze the stamens together between your fingers and flatten them slightly, leaving enough of the stamens unglued to make them appear natural. Allow to set slightly and then cut the stamens shorter.

Glue the six groups around the ovary, squeezing them together in order to help them stick. However, only do this when you are confident that the paste

ovary is completely dry, otherwise the glue will dissolve the sugar.

3 Dust the tips with a mixture of primrose and lemon, and dust the the filaments with scarlet craft dust. Curl the stamens out slightly using tweezers.

petals

4 Squash the large rose petal cutters into the shape of the templates on page 155. Roll out some melon-coloured flower paste, leaving a thick ridge at the centre. Cut out five to fifteen petals using various sizes of cutters. The flower pictured on page 77 has been made with the largest cutter and the flower pictured on the drift wood on page 81 has been made with the large and medium cutters.

5 Insert a moistened 26-gauge wire into the base of each petal. Vein and frill the upper curved edge of each petal with the silk veining tool. Stretch the centre of the petals with your fingers and thumb, and allow to dry in an apple tray former.

colouring & assembly

6 Dust each petal from the base with a mixture of primrose and lemon dusting powders. Then dust a patch of scarlet at the base of each petal. Tape the petals tightly around the stamens, overlapping where necessary. If you are making a double peony, the smallest petals should be taped around the stamens first, followed by the larger petals. The aim is to position a petal over a join in the first layer.

calyx

7 The calyx is made up from three rounded sepals and two longer, narrow sepals. Roll out some green paste on to a grooved board and cut out three graduating sizes of rose petal cutters to represent the sepals. Insert a moistened 30-gauge wire into the pointed end of each sepal. Soften the edges and hollow them out slightly. Pinch a tiny point in the rounded end of each sepal.

8 Roll a teardrop piece of mid-holly/ivy paste and insert a 30-gauge wire into the broad end. Thin the teardrop between your fingers and then smooth between your palms to form a neat point. Place the shape on the board and flatten the sepal using the flat side of the veining tool. Pinch the length of the sepal to create a central vein.

Repeat to make two long sepals. Dust both the rounded and long sepals with vine green and holly/ivy powders.

9 Tape the three rounded sepals (evenly spaced) behind the flower, followed by the long, narrow ones. Bend the two long sepals back slightly.

buds

10 Bend a large hook in the end of a piece of 18-gauge white wire. Roll a medium to large ball of pale melon paste and insert the moistened, hooked wire in at one end. Allow to dry.

11 Cut out five petal shapes using the smallest rose petal cutter or template. Vein and frill as for the flower. Moisten each petal with egg white and attach them to the dried base. Crease the petals when they are in position to create a tight bud.

12 Dust as for the flower and then attach a calyx. This time the three rounded sepals are unwired but you will need to wire the two long ones.

leaves

13 Roll out some mid-green flower paste, leaving a thick ridge at the centre. Cut out a leaf shape using one of the peony leaf cutters or templates from page 155. Insert a moistened wire – you can use anything from a 28- to a 24-gauge white wire depending on the size of the leaf.

Soften the edges and vein each section of the leaf with the single peony leaf veiner. Pinch the leaf to reinforce the central vein and pinch the tip into a neat point. Repeat this process to make the total number of required leaves.

14 Dust the edges of each leaf with aubergine and then overdust the main body of the leaf with forest green, holly/ivy and lots of vine green dusting powders. Allow to dry a little more and then dip into a 1/2 glaze.

15 Tape two or three sets of small leaves behind each bud and flower. Every time you join two stems together, tape in a set of larger leaves at the junction. Dust the stems with aubergine and holly/ivy dusting powders.

Autumn Wedding Cake

This autumnal wedding cake was created to celebrate the marriage of my friend Alice's daughter, and was partly inspired by a Celtic design. It is made from polystyrene – the real cake was simply iced, cut into individual slices and wrapped in wax paper, with gold tissue paper and a tied bow. The slices were then stored in a drawer, which was part of the base stand. The couple cut the ribbon on the drawer handle, rather than the cake itself, and the drawer was opened to reveal a slice of cake for each guest!

cake & decoration

25cm (10in) and 30cm (12in) teardrop-
shaped polystyrene dummy cakes or
25cm (10in) polystyrene dummy
and 30cm (12in) rich fruit cake
Apricot glaze
3kg (6lb) white almond paste (marzipan)
Clear alcohol (kirsch, white rum,
cointreau etc)
3.5kg (7lb) champagne sugarpaste
(rolled fondant)
Fine and broad samion ribbon to trim
the cakes and edge of the boards
Gold metallic powders
Forest green and foliage green
dusting powders (petal dust/blossom tint)

◆

equipment

Sugarpaste smoothers
30cm (12in) teardrop-shaped cake board
40cm (16in) oval cake board
Long, tilting, perspex cake stand [C]
Short length of right-angled plastic
Strong bonding glue and non-toxic
glue stick
Greaseproof paper
Fine celpick
Tall, twisted candleholder
Florists' green staysoft or a small block
of dry oasis
Crystal pillar [W]

◆

flowers

2 Autumn Wedding Bouquets plus two
smaller sprays of roses (see p.84)

preparation

1 Brush the cake with apricot glaze, cover with almond paste and leave to dry. Moisten both the dummy cake and the real cake with clear alcohol, and cover them with champagne sugarpaste. Use the smoothers to achieve a good finish. Cover the boards with sugarpaste and transfer the cakes on top.

2 Attach a band of fine samion ribbon to the the base of both cakes. Glue the broad ribbon to the edge of the board using the non-toxic glue.

side design

3 Using the template on page 156, trace the design on to a piece of greaseproof paper and then scribe the design on to each of the cakes. Paint in the design using the mixed gold powders diluted with clear alcohol. Outline the design with the forest and foliage green dusting powders.

4 Glue the piece of right-angled plastic (plastic edging) to the underside of the top tier using a strong glue. The plastic will enable you simply to hook the cake on top of the perspex stand, preventing the risk of the cake moving!

assembly

5 Insert a small spray of roses into the top tier using a fine celpick. Fill the candle holder with staysoft and insert a bouquet into it. Position the candle holder next to the tilted top tier. Place the larger tier at the base. (It may pay to place a smaller cake board under the base cake, to help lift it up slightly.) Insert the crystal pillar into the base tier and insert a slightly larger bouquet into that. Finish by adding a rose spray to the base of the tier.

Autumn Wedding Bouquet

The flowers used in the sprays on the Autumn Wedding Cake were those carried
by Alice's daughter, Jean. She also carried love-lies-bleeding and miniature red nerines; the latter was
a surprise to everyone, including the bride, and the former was too tricky to produce in sugar to any
great effect, so we (Alice and I) opted to leave it out! Jean's coffee-gold wedding dress made
a wonderful back-drop to this stunning colour scheme.

flowers

9 stems of eucalyptus (see p.72)
1 full rose, 2 rose buds and 3 half roses
(see p.136 of *Floral Wedding Cakes & Sprays*)
3 arum lilies (see p.88)
5 stems of hypericum berries (see p.78 of
Floral Wedding Cakes & Sprays)
3 stems of bupleurum (see p.89)
10 stems of rosemary (see p.65 of
Floral Wedding Cakes & Sprays)

◆

equipment

20- and 18-gauge wire
Fine-nosed pliers
Wire cutters
Nile green floristry tape

preparation

1 Any weak or short flower stems can
be elongated and strengthened by
taping additional 20- or 18-gauge wire
alongside the main stems.

assembly

2 First, decide how long the bouquet
needs to be. The first stem of
eucalyptus should measure at least two-
thirds the total length of the bouquet.
Bend the stem to a 90-degree angle.
Next, add another piece of eucalyptus
to form at least another one-third of the
bouquet. Bend the stem of this piece and
tape it on to the longer piece of foliage.
These two pieces of foliage will now
form the basic curved shape and length
of the bouquet.
Continue to add shorter stems of
eucalyptus in the same way, until you have
have formed an almost complete outline
of the bouquet shape.

3 Next, wire the full rose into the
centre of the bouquet to act as the
main focal point. (This should be slightly
higher than any of the other flowers that
are to be added to the bouquet.)
Join the three half roses around the
full rose. Tape in two rose buds at the
tip of the bouquet.

4 Tape in the three arum lilies. Use
the curves already outlined by the
eucalyptus leaves as a guide for
positioning these flowers. Finally, fill
in the gaps in the bouquet with the
hypericum berries and bupleurum.
For a slightly wild edge to the
bouquet, try adding plenty of rosemary.
Stand back from the display and make
any necessary adjustments.

leonardis rose

The leonardis rose (*Rosa*
'Leonardis') used here was made
from pale melon paste. This was
coated with a mixture of plum
and tangerine dusting powders
and then overdusted with
aubergine dusting powder. The
backs of each petal were dusted
with a mixture of white, lemon
and primrose powders.

Autumn Wedding Arrangement

This arrangement is a continuation of the flowers used with the cake on page 82. Orange and blue flowers work wonderfully well together and are used here alongside the brown leonardis rose (page 84) to create a very majestic display. Although many people think of roses as quite normal, rather than exotic, we would not have the variety in colour and shape without the imports of flowers from China and India.

flowers

3 full roses, 7 half roses and 7 rose buds
(see p.136 of *Floral Wedding Cakes & Sprays*)
9 arum lilies (p.88)
10 stems of eucalyptus leaves (p.72)
3 stems of flaming trumpet vine (p.110)
3 trailing stems of blue glory bower (p.40)
7 stems of hypericum berries (see p.78 of
Floral Wedding Cakes & Sprays)
12 stems of rosemary (see p.65 of *Floral
Wedding Cakes & Sprays*)

◆

equipment

18-gauge wire
Fine-nosed pliers and wire cutters
Nile green floristry tape
Florists' green staysoft or a small block
of dry oasis
20cm (8in) diameter green dish
Non-toxic high-tack craft glue

preparation

1 Strengthen any flower stems that may seem weak by taping additional 18-gauge wires alongside the main stems. Attach a piece of florists' staysoft into the base of the green dish using a small amount of non-toxic glue.

assembly

2 Bend a hook in the end of each of the rose stems to provide further support. Insert the roses into the staysoft using the largest rose that you have as the focal flower. Next, add the stems of the arum lilies to provide height and shape to the arrangement.

3 Start to add the eucalyptus leaves to fill the outline of the shape. Add the three stems of flaming trumpet vine. Next, carefully insert the stems of blue glory bower, curving them to create an interesting shape.

4 Finally, add the hypericum berries and plenty of rosemary stems. Use the pliers to position the stems into the staysoft. Stand back from the display, and make any adjustments required.

Arum Lily
(Zantedeschia aethiopica)

Arum lilies sometimes called 'calla' are from Africa, but have been cultivated in Europe since 1687. The colour variation includes white, yellow, pink, orange, green, red, burgundy and almost black. Although occasionally considered to be funeral flowers, they are now used more often in bridal bouquets.

materials

Pale melon flower paste
(gum paste)
18-gauge wire
Egg white
Aubergine, lemon, tangerine, plum, red, vine green and holly/ivy dusting powders
(petal dust/blossom tint)
Mimosa yellow sugartex
Kitchen paper
Nile green floristry tape

◆

equipment

Sharp scalpel
Extra large amaryllis veiner [GI]
Arum lily template (see p.156)
Dresden veining tool
Foam pad

spadix

1 Roll a medium-sized ball of well-kneaded pale melon flower paste and then insert an 18-gauge wire into it. Work the paste quickly and firmly between your fingers and thumb to cover a length of about 4.5cm (1¾in) of the wire.

Smooth the shape between your palms and remove any excess paste. Attach a ball of paste to the base of the spadix to give more padding to the finished flower.

2 Dust the spadix with aubergine dusting powder. Paint the surface with fresh egg white and then roll it in yellow sugartex. Allow to dry.

spathe

3 Roll out some pale melon flower paste, though be careful not to make it too thin. Place the spathe template on top of the paste and cut around it using a sharp scalpel.

Vein the spathe with the large amaryllis veiner. Put the spathe on a pad and soften the edges. Using the fine end of the dresden veining tool, add some extra central veins.

4 Moisten the base of the spathe. Then place the spadix on either the left or right side (they seem to grow on both). Gently roll the two together, taking care not to get any 'pollen' on to the spathe.

Curl back the edges, particularly the long edge that overlaps. Pinch the tip into a very fine point and leave to dry upside down until the paste is firm enough to dust.

5 Thicken the stem with more 18-gauge wire, shredded kitchen paper and nile green floristry tape.

colouring

6 The flower pictured here has been dusted with tangerine, lemon, plum, red and aubergine dusting powders. The base and tips of the flower were dusted with a mixture of vine green and holly/ivy. Once the flower is dry, steam it to help set the colour.

Bupleurum
(Bupleurum griffithii)

Bupleurum – sorry, it does not seem to have a common name – is native to Southern Europe and, while the flowers are not difficult to make, they do require patience and time! This green-flowered herb is used extensively by florists as both a flower and foliage filler. Only flowers were used on the Autumn Wedding Cake (see page 82), as the bouquet design did not need the leaves. The flowers are actually what would initially be considered to be the stamens and the bracts look like green pointed petals.

materials

Non-toxic craft glue
Tiny-headed stamens
32- and 22-gauge wire
Primrose, lemon, vine green, forest green, moss green and holly/ivy dusting powders (petal dust/blossom tint)
Pale and mid-green flower paste (gum paste)
Egg white
Nile green floristry tape
¼ glaze

◆

equipment

Small calyx cutter [TT 406, 304, 526]
Dresden veining tool
Celstick

stamens (flowers)

1 Glue about ten, tiny-headed stamens on to the end of a short piece of 32-gauge wire. Repeat to make the required number of centres. Leave to dry before dusting with primrose and lemon powders.

flowers (bracts)

2 Roll out a small ball of paste leaving a pimple at the centre. Cut out one of the three sizes of calyx shape – you will need to use all three to complete a stem. Lengthen three of the petals along one side of the shape. Soften the edges and then vein the centre of each petal using the fine end of the dresden veining tool. Moisten the base of the stamens with fresh egg white and thread through the centre of the calyx shape. Allow to firm a little before dusting. Repeat to make as many flower heads as you require. Tape over each stem with quarter width nile green floristry tape.

colouring

3 Dust each flower shape with vine green dusting powder and then overdust with a touch of moss green. Tape the flowers tightly together to form small florets, using quarter width floristry tape.

assembly & leaves

4 Tape together two sets of florets to a 22-gauge wire. Roll out some mid-green paste, leaving a pimple at the centre, and cut out one of the sizes of rose petal shape. Soften the edges and open the centre using the pointed end of the celstick. Using the fine end of the veining tool, create several lines radiating from the centre. Moisten the join below the point where the two sets of flowers have been taped and then thread the leaf shape over the top to cover the join. Repeat this process as many times as required but increase the size of the leaf shapes as you gradually work down the stem. When complete, allow the sugarpaste to dry before dusting with forest green and holly/ivy dusting powders. Apply a ¼ glaze.

Viridiflora Cake

Green has always been my favourite colour and here I have used green pineapple lilies, cockleshell orchids, burgundy-striped green amaryllis and caladium leaves. Although the main flowers in each spray are different, they have been linked together by using ruscus and hypericum berries to create this very unusual, single-tiered cake. The green theme even makes the cake suitable as a Christmas alternative.

cake & decoration

17.5cm (7in) round-shaped rich fruit cake
Apricot glaze
500g (1lb) white almond paste (marzipan)
Clear alcohol (kirsch, white rum, cointreau etc)
750g (1½lb) white sugarpaste (rolled fondant)
Broad white organza-type ribbon to trim the edge of the cake

◆

equipment

Sugarpaste smoothers
17.5cm (7in) round, thin cake board
Strong bonding glue (suitable for paper, wood or plastic)
Short length of right-angled plastic
Fine-nosed pliers and wire cutters
Nile green floristry tape
Perspex tilting cake stand
Plastic posy pick

◆

flowers

top spray:
2 stems of ruscus (see p.107)
2 amaryllis flowers, plus five buds (see p.94)
3 caladium leaves (see p.97)
4 small stems of bupleurum (see p.89)
2 stems of hypericum berries (see below)
bottom spray:
2 stems of pineapple flowers (see p.98)
2 cockleshell orchids, plus 3 buds (see p.100)
2 stems of ruscus (see p.107)
2 small stems of bupleurum (see p.89)
3 stems of hypericum berries (see p.78 of *Floral Wedding Cakes & Sprays*)

preparation

1 Position the cake on top of the board and brush with apricot glaze.

Cover both the cake and the edge of the board with almond paste. Allow the paste to dry before moistening the surface with clear alcohol. Cover the cake and edge of the board with white sugarpaste and leave them aside for a few hours to dry.

2 Glue a short length of right-angled plastic on to the base of the cake board and allow to dry. This can then be hooked over the edge of the tilting stand to hold the cake in place.

top spray assembly

3 To form the basic shape of the top spray, bend and tape together the two stems of ruscus at a 90-degree angle. Next, add the amaryllis flowers and buds, so that they form the focal point of the spray. Continue building the shape by adding the caladium leaves, hypericum berries and bupleurum flowers.

Cut away any excess wires and tape over to neaten the handle of the spray. Insert the handle into a posy pick and then insert this into the top of the cake.

bottom spray assembly

4 Form a tied bunch and tape the stems together at one point. Bend the stems to frame the base of the cake display. Position next to the cake as pictured here.

Simple Contemporary Arrangements

It is not always necessary to have large numbers of flowers and foliage to create stunning designs. In fact, sometimes just a few stems arranged in a vase, or a collection of complementary flowers simply positioned together, can be enough to demonstrate your flower-making techniques. These contemporary arrangements achieve their style through their simplicity.

above: Two stems of pineapple flowers (page 98) and a single caladium leaf (page 97) have been
set in a misted glass vase to create a very stylized, modern arrangement.
opposite: A collection of green-flowered plants have been grouped together and arranged in a small misted
glass vase. The container is filled with sea salt to help support the flowers and hide the stems.

Amaryllis

Sometimes known as *Hippeastrum*, amaryllis originate from the tropical and subtropical rainforests of South America and the Caribbean. They are usually grown as pot plants, but are now becoming increasingly popular as cut flowers too. In fact, they make stunning focal flowers for bridal bouquets. The flower pictured here is based on a variety called 'Papillion'. This variety would make a wonderful alternative flower for a Christmas cake or display.

<table>
<tr><td>

materials

26-, 24-, 20- and 18-gauge white wire
White and nile green floristry tape
Pale green and white flower paste
(gum paste)
Vine green, dark green, moss, aubergine
and plum dusting powders
(petal dust/blossom tint)
Cyclamen liquid colour [SK]
Kitchen paper

</td><td>

equipment

Fine-nosed pliers
Sharp scalpel and sharp scissors
Grooved board (optional)
Amaryllis templates (see p.156) or
cutters [TT]
Large wide amaryllis petal veiner [GI]
Large celstick
Dresden veining tool
Fine and broad paintbrushes

</td></tr>
</table>

stamens

1 Cut two lengths of 26-gauge white wire into thirds. Using a pair of fine-nosed pliers, bend a flat hook at one end of the wire. Hold the hook half way down its length with the pliers and bend it again to form a T-bar shape.

Thicken the length of each stamen either with quarter width white floristry tape or with well-kneaded white flower paste, making sure that they are finer towards the anther. Curve the length of the stamen before the paste begins to dry out.

2 Attach a small sausage of white paste over the T-bars to form the anthers. (You will not need to use egg white for this.) The size of the anther depends upon the maturity of the flower – a mature flower would have smaller anthers. Using a sharp scalpel, indent a line on to the upper surface of the anther. Dust the length of the stamen with vine green dusting powder.

pistil

3 Roll a ball of pale green paste and insert a dry 24-gauge white wire. Work the paste firmly and quickly between your finger and thumb to cover a good length of the wire. The pistil should not be longer than the petals. Smooth the pistil between the palms of your hands and trim off the excess paste. Use a small pair of scissors to cut the end of the pistil into three sections. Round off the sides of each of the sections, then curl them back a little. Bend the whole length of the pistil into a very lazy S-shape. Dust the pistil with vine green powder and allow to dry.

4 Tape the six stamens on to the pistil using half width green floristry tape, making sure that the pistil is a little longer. Tape on to an 18-gauge wire.

petals

5 Roll out some pale green paste or your chosen colour paste, leaving a thick ridge down the centre. (Alternatively, use a grooved board.) Cut out the two medium-sized petals and one central, narrow petal using the templates on page 156. This should produce a left, right and central petal.

6 Insert a moistened 26-gauge wire into the thick ridge of each petal, making sure that the wire supports at least half the length of the petals. Broaden the two side petals slightly using a rolling action with the length of a celstick. Use the straight veins on the large amaryllis veiner to vein each of the petals and then soften the edges with the rounded end of the celstick, but do not make them too frilly.

7 Pinch each petal at the tips and at the base. On some petals, curl the edges at the base slightly, to add visual interest and give some variation.

Allow the sugarpaste to firm slightly before dusting and assembling the flower.

sepals

8 Repeat the process to make three outer sepals using either the largest petal shape or the medium-sized petal cutter (this will depend upon which variety you are making). You will need to wire the larger petals with 24-gauge wire to give them enough support.

Vein the sepals with the upper section of the large amaryllis veiner. Soften the edges and then draw down a central vein using the fine end of the dresden tool. Pinch the tips and the base of the sepals and allow the paste to firm up with a slight curve.

colouring & assembly

9 Dust each petal with vine green and then overdust with a small amount of moss green dusting powder. Work from the base of each petal and

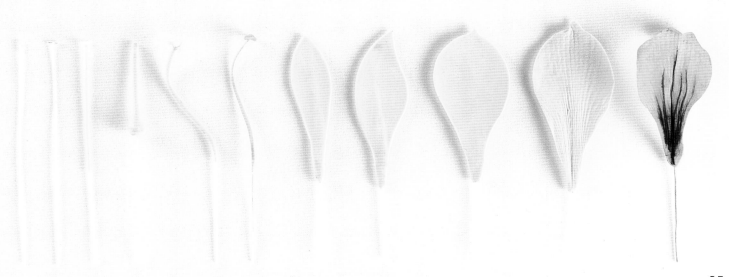

95

add a small amount of colour to the edges and tips.

10 Using a fine paintbrush and cyclamen liquid colour, paint a striped design on to each of the petals and sepals, creating heavier markings on the two side petals. Remember to paint the backs as well. Use a broader brush to catch the edge of each of the petals with the cyclamen colouring. Then overdust the lines with a mixture of plum and aubergine dusting powders.

11 Tape the left and right petals on to the stamens, so that the stamens curl towards them. Add the narrow petal underneath the stamens. Position the three outer sepals behind and in between each of the petals, and tape the flower together tightly using half width nile green floristry tape.

If your petals are still soft, use this to your advantage by adjusting their positions to create a natural, relaxed shape. Thicken the stem with shredded kitchen paper and some full width nile green floristry tape.

buds

12 Bend a large hook in the end of a 20- or 18-gauge wire. Roll a large ball of green paste into a torpedo shape and insert the moistened wire into the fine end.

Divide the bud into three sections using a sharp scalpel. Then use the same scalpel to create fine veins on each of the divisions, twisting the tip slightly. Make several buds for each stem; try graduating sizes for greater effect.

13 Dust the buds with vine green, moss green, plum and aubergine powders. Add cyclamen lines and thicken the stems, using the same technique as you did for the flower.

assembly

14 Thicken the flower and bud stems with kitchen paper and then tape over with full width nile green floristry tape. Group the flowers and buds into groups of a maximum of five. Coat the stems with dark green, vine and moss dusting powders.

Caladium

Caladiums originate from Central America and northern regions of South America. Their leaves can be very large, despite the fact that they have a very fine, delicate texture. The plants can produce very simply coloured red and green leaves, as well as highly decorative green veins on white, cream and pink leaves. These plants are ideal for adding interest to a sugarcraft display, and are an excellent means of filling space in a large arrangement or spray.

materials

White or ivory flower paste (gum paste)
20-gauge white wire
Forest green, vine green and holly/ivy dusting powders
(petal dust/blossom tint)
Isopropyl alcohol
1/4 glaze
Nile green floristry tape

◆

equipment

Syngonium leaf cutters, optional [CC]
Plain edge cutting wheel [PME]
or sharp scalpel
Foam pad
Fresh caladium leaf, caladium veiner [GI] or veining tool
Fine and larger flat paintbrushes

leaves

1 Roll out a large piece of white flower paste, leaving a thick ridge at the centre. Use a syngonium leaf cutter to cut out the leaf shape or, alternatively, use the cutting wheel or a sharp scalpel for a freehand leaf shape.

2 Insert a moistened 20-gauge white wire into the thick ridge. Place the leaf on a pad and soften the edges gently but do not frill.

3 Using either a fresh leaf, caladium veiner or veining tool, create a textured surface to the leaf. If you are using the veining tool, begin with a main central Y-shaped vein and then add finer veins. Pinch the leaf down the centre and then allow to firm before dusting and painting.

colouring

4 Mix together forest green, vine green and holly/ivy dusting powders with some isopropyl alcohol to form a solid paint. Use a fine paintbrush to paint in the main Y-shaped vein, followed by the finer veins. (You will need to keep adding alcohol to keep the paint flowing.) Paint a line just inside the edge of the leaf to create a border, and then use a larger, flat brush to paint from the edge, up to the border. Allow to dry.

5 Dust the leaf from the edges and the centre with vine green. The larger the leaf, the less green it will be. Dip the paste into a 1/4 glaze or simply steam to set the colours. Thicken the stem with further nile green tape. If the leaf is very large, ensure that enough wire is added to support its weight.

Pineapple Flower
(*Eucomis autumnalis*)

The fifteen species of *Eucomis* originate from South Africa and were first introduced into Europe in 1760. As the Latin name implies, this is an autumn-flowering plant and its common name is due to its pineapple-like tufts of leaves at the top of each flower spike. In fact its genus name, translated from Greek, means 'with a lovely crest'. It can be good fun to actually wire these flowers together to form a more rounded pineapple-shaped flower head, instead of the straight spike pictured below. This is a very simple flower to make; however, you will need time and lots of patience to produce large quantities!

materials

28-, 26- and 18-gauge white wire
White, pale green and mid-holly/ivy flower paste (gum paste)
Vine green, primrose, aubergine, deep purple and holly/ivy dusting powders (petal dust/blossom tint)
Small white seed-head stamens
Non-toxic high-tack craft glue
Nile green floristry tape
Egg white
Isopropyl alcohol
½ glaze

◆

equipment

Fine-nosed pliers
Grooved board
Medium celstick
Six-petalled blossom cutters
[OPN 4, 5, 6]
Dresden veining tool
Broad, flat paintbrush
Bittersweet leaf veiner [GI]

ovary and stamens

1 Bend a small hook in the end of a short length of 26-gauge wire. Roll a small ball of pale green paste into a cone shape. Insert the hooked wire into the broad base of the cone. Pinch the cone shape with your fingers to create three sides to the ovary. Pinch the tip firmly to produce a sharp point before dusting with vine green dusting powder. Allow the paste to dry.

2 Use a small amount of non-toxic glue to attach six short, white seed-head stamens around the ovary. (Make sure that the paste is dry, otherwise the sugar centre may dissolve.) Alternatively, tape the stamens around the ovary with quarter width floristry tape. Dust the tips with either primrose or aubergine dusting powder (depending on your chosen variety).

flower

3 Roll a ball of white or pale green paste into a cone shape. Pinch the broad end between your fingers and thumb to form a pedestal shape. Put the flat end against the board and roll it out using a celstick, to form a neat waistline around the base of the pedestal.

4 Cut out the flower shape using one of the three sizes of blossom cutter. Place the flower flat-side down on the board and lengthen each of the petals slightly using the celstick.

5 Open up the throat of the flower using the pointed end of the celstick. Put the flower over your index finger and use the dresden veining tool to hollow out and vein the length of each petal.

Gently pinch the tips of each petal between your finger and thumb. Pinch the three alternate petals a little more than the other three, to create the character of the flower.

6 Moisten the base of the stamens with egg white and pull through the centre of the flower so that it sits snugly in the centre. Neaten the back of the flower and remove any excess paste. Repeat this process to make plenty of flowers; there are about 30 on the stem pictured, but the real plant has many more!

colouring

7 The simplest *Eucomis* is the white-flowered variety as it needs only a small amount of vine green dust added to the back of each flower. The stem pictured has been dusted lightly with vine green dusting powder and then the edges finished with aubergine and deep purple mixed together. For a more definite edge, dilute some colour and just catch the edges of the petals with the tip of a broad, flat paintbrush.

buds

8 The buds are very quick to make and can help to fill a long stem that would otherwise require numerous flowers! To make them, hook and moisten the end of a short length of 28- or 26-gauge wire. Roll a small ball of paste into a sharp pointed cone and insert the wire into the broad end.

Work the base of the cone to stretch the back of the bud and form a long slender neck. Pinch the end of the bud with your fingers and thumb to create three sides to the bud, each with sharp ridges. Dust in the same way as the flower, catching the ridges with aubergine to create definite lines. Repeat to make your required number in various graduating sizes.

crest leaves

9 Roll out some mid-green paste on a grooved board and cut out a basic pointed leaf shape using the cutting wheel. Insert a moistened 28-gauge wire into the thick ridge. Place the leaf on a pad and soften the edges. Vein using the bittersweet leaf veiner.

Pinch the leaf from the base to the tip to accentuate the central vein. Repeat to make 15–20 leaves of various sizes. Dust the main leaf area with vine green and holly/ivy dusting powder and then dust or paint the edges with aubergine. Allow to dry or dip into a ½ glaze.

assembly

10 Tape a crest of leaves on to the end of three 18-gauge wires. Start to add the buds in among the leaves, then continue using only the buds by themselves. (On a real stem, each bud and flower has a slim, small bract at the base – this sugar version does not.)

Continue down the stem, taping in some small flowers using half or even full width tape to create a very fleshy stem. Start to add the larger flowers until you have covered the length of stem you require.

11 The variety shown here has aubergine-spotted stems (those of you who know me will be aware of my love of aubergine colourings!) Dilute some more aubergine dusting powder with isopropyl alcohol and then paint uneven spots over the stem, dodging in between each of the flowers. If you wish, paint the stem carefully with ½ glaze in order to seal the colour on the stem.

note

The leaves at the base of the plant are very large and are not suitable for use on cakes. They often have very wavy edges and lots of aubergine spots, although this can vary considerably between different varieties.

Cockleshell Orchid
(Encyclia cochleata)

This orchid acquired its name through its shell-like lip petal. However, it is also sometimes known as the 'octopus orchid' because of its long, dangling petals. It originates from South America and the West Indies, and it was the first epiphytic orchid to flower in Britain at the Royal Botanical Gardens in Kew, in 1763. I have recently seen a similar variety with a pink upper lip and pure white hanging petals; so if you are not a big fan of green orchids then perhaps the alternative might interest you.

---

materials

28-, 24- and 20-gauge white wire
Very pale and mid-green flower paste
(gum paste)
Egg white
Vine green, primrose, lemon, dark green, holly/ivy and aubergine dusting powders (petal dust/blossom tint)
Cyclamen liquid food colour

◆

equipment

Sharp scissors
Sharp scalpel
Flower templates (see p.157)
Ceramic silk veining tool
Dendrobium lip veiner (optional)
Foam pad
Small ball tool
Plain edge cutting wheel [PME]
Dresden veining tool

---

column

1 Bend a small hook in the end of a piece of 24-gauge white wire. Roll a small ball of pale green flower paste into a cone shape. Insert the moistened, hooked wire into the narrow end of the cone and work the paste firmly between your finger and thumb to elongate the shape a little.

2 Hollow out the underside of the column so that it looks a bit like a cobra. Use a fine pair of sharp scissors to make two slanted cuts into the tip of the column. Indent between each of the cuts with the scalpel and then round off the two pieces of paste and pull them together to form an anther cap. Leave aside to dry.

throat petal (labellum)

3 Roll out a small piece of pale green paste, leaving a ridge at the centre (this petal is not wired, but it helps to give the flower some support if a ridge is used). Place the throat petal template on top of the paste and cut out the shape using a sharp scalpel.

4 Vein the petal either by using the silk veining tool in a fan formation or by using the dendrobium lip veiner. Frill the edge of the petal a little with the silk veining tool. Do not frill the petal too much. Place the petal on a pad and use a small ball tool to hollow out the petal on either side of the main central veins.

5 Moisten the base of the petal with a little fresh egg white and position the dried column on top. Wrap the lip petal around the column and then curl the edges back slightly. Allow to dry a little before colouring.

outer petals & sepals

6 There are two very narrow wing petals and three longer outer sepals (which are all made in the same way). Roll out a narrow piece of mid-green paste very thinly, leaving a thick ridge. Use one of the petal template shapes and the cutting wheel to cut out a petal shape. Once you get used to the length and thickness of the petals they can be cut out freehand using the cutting wheel. Insert a moistened 28-gauge wire into each.

7 Soften the edges of the petal and then draw down a central vein using either the fine end of the dresden tool or the small end of the cutting wheel. Pinch the tip firmly and add curls to the end. Repeat to make five outer petals.

buds

8 Roll a ball of well-kneaded, pale green paste into a long slender teardrop-shape. Insert a hooked, moistened 24-gauge white wire into the base. Smooth the shape down and divide the surface into five sections using a scalpel. Curve the tip gracefully.

colouring & assembly

9 Dust the buds and the long, outer petals with vine green dusting powder, fading the colour out towards the tips. Dust a mixture of primrose and lemon dusting powders into the heart of the throat petal and then dust the edges towards the centre with aubergine.

The markings on the lip are quite complicated so I have simplified them for this sugar version. Paint some veins in from the edge of the throat with the cyclamen food colour and a fine brush. Add some spots to the column and some central lines on the inside of the petal.

Protea Arrangement

These stunning proteas were made by my friend Tombi Peck, who kindly allowed me to use them in this book! I have arranged them with ruscus foliage and a few stems of Queen's tears. These flowers are large and are ideal for use on their own because they create such a good impact.

flowers

3 large protea flowers and
2 protea buds (see p.104)
9 stems of ruscus (see p.107)
3 stems of Queen's tears (see p.28)

◆

equipment

Florists' green staysoft or a small block
of dry oasis
Oval wooden bowl or similar
Non-toxic high-tack craft glue
18-gauge wire
Fine-nosed pliers and wire cutters
Nile green floristry tape

preparation

1 Fix a large piece of florists' staysoft or dry oasis into the wooden bowl with the glue. Strengthen any weak flower and foliage stems by attaching some 18-gauge wire with floristry tape.

assembly

2 Gently bend hooks in the ends of each of the proteas – this will help them to stay in position. Insert each of the hooked proteas into the staysoft, so that they form the bulk of the arrangement.

3 Trim the lengths of the ruscus stems to the required height. As with the protea, hook the ends and then begin to insert them into the staysoft. The ruscus should form the outline of the arrangement and fill in any obvious gaps.

4 Hook the ends of the Queen's tears stems and carefully insert them into the edges of the arrangement. Stand back from the display and take some time to re-adjust the flower positions until you are happy with the effect.

Protea

Proteas are named after the Greek god Proteus, who had the ability to change his shape and take on many forms. Proteas can be trees or shrubs, with some displaying a low, tufted growth. The flower and leaf shapes vary a lot, as does the colour. The flower described here is based on *Protea compacta*. Proteas are mostly found in South Africa and Australia.

stamen centre

1 Sculpt the styrofoam ball or egg shape so that it has a slight point at the tip. Bend a large hook in the end of a piece of 14-gauge wire.

Apply some glue to the hook and then insert it into the styrofoam. Leave both the wire and styrofoam aside for a few hours to dry.

2 Soften some white flower paste and extrude it through the fine mesh in the sugar shaper. Gradually apply the strands of paste to the moistened base. As you obtain the required length of stamen paste, pull it away from the sugar shaper to form tapered tips. You will find that the strands break off at different lengths but this helps to create the right finish. Press the sides of the centre to get the strands to stick to it. Then indent the tip of the stamen centre to create a recessed look. Trim off the excess paste and allow to dry.

3 Take a bunch of lily stamens and glue them into smaller groups before flattening the sides.

materials

Styrofoam ball or egg (for the centre)
28-, 26-, 24-, and 22-gauge
white wire and 14-gauge green wire
Non-toxic high-tack craft glue
White and pale holly/ivy flower paste
(gum paste)
Pale yellow, large, straight-tipped lily
stamens
White, vine green, holly/ivy, dark green,
daffodil and aubergine dusting powders
(petal dust/blossom tint)
Isopropyl alcohol
Deep magenta craft dust
Nile green floristry tape
Kitchen paper
$^1/_4$ or $^1/_2$ glaze

◆

equipment

Sugar shaper clay gun
Cattleya orchid sepal cutters,
two sizes [J]
Small ball tool
King protea cutters, three sizes [J]
Dresden veining tool
Sharp scalpel
Small and large protea leaf veiners [GI]

Add some lengths of stamen that do not have tips. Allow these to dry and attach them to the dried centre using either softened flower paste or some more non-toxic glue. (Check that glue is permissible if the flowers are being entered in a competition.) Press the stamens firmly against the centre of the glue to secure them into place.

4 Dust the filaments with daffodil and vine green dusting powders. The anthers are dusted with deep magenta and the top of the paste stamens are dusted with a circle of deep magenta.
Darken the very centre with aubergine dusting powder. Dilute some white dusting powder with alcohol and use this mixture to paint a ring on the tips of the paste stamens.

petals

5 Roll out some white paste, leaving a thick ridge. Cut out a large petal using the large cattleya orchid cutter. Insert a moistened 26-gauge wire into the thick ridge. Soften the edges of the petal using

a ball tool and then hollow out the length. Repeat this process to make 20–25 large petals and 16–18 smaller ones. (The number will depend upon the size of the flower required.)

colouring & assembly

6 Dust each petal with vine green at the base. Cover the main body of each petal with deep magenta craft dust, leaving the tips paler (almost white).

7 Tape the larger petals around the centre, and then add the smaller ones. Press the petals firmly against the centre before they have a chance to dry completely – this will distinguish a good flower paste from a bad one! The petals should fit over a join in each layer.

calyx

8 Roll out some green paste, leaving a thick ridge in the middle. Cut out a sepal shape using one of the three sizes of king protea petal cutters. Insert

a 28-gauge wire into the thick ridge. Soften the edges and then draw down a strong central vein using a dresden tool. Pinch the tip into a sharp point. Repeat this process to make between 20–25 sepals of various sizes.

9 Gently dust the edges of each sepal with aubergine and deep magenta powders. Overdust the whole of each sepal with dark green, holly/ivy and white dusting powders. Tape the calyx on to the base of the flower using the same method as for the petals.

10 Thicken the stem with some shredded kitchen paper and full width nile green floristry tape.

bud

11 The bud is also made from styrofoam that has been carved into an oval shape. However, this time the petals are simply attached, unwired, to the base.
Use the smaller petal cutter to cut out several petals. Position each petal over a

join in the first layer. Make a calyx in the same way as you did for the flower, using the smaller protea cutters. Dust the bud following the same techniques as used for the flower.

leaves

12 Roll out some green paste, leaving a thick ridge. Press the back of one of the leaf veiners into the paste to leave an outline. Cut out the leaf shape using a sharp scalpel and insert a moistened 26-, 24- or 22-gauge white wire, depending upon the size of leaf. Position the leaf on a pad and gently soften the edges.

13 Vein the paste using the protea double-sided leaf veiner. Pinch the leaf from the base to the tip, to help emphasize the central vein. Repeat to make leaves of various sizes.

colouring

14 Dust the edges of the leaves with aubergine and deep magenta. Dust the main body of the leaf with dark green, holly/ivy and lots of white dusting powders. Dip the paste into a $1/4$ or $1/2$ glaze depending upon your taste. Tape the leaves on to the main stem. Dust the stem with the various colours used on the leaves.

Ruscus

Although ruscus is not an exotic foliage, it is very useful as a companion to many exotic flowers and there are many varieties. Interestingly, the small nodules that appear to be leaves are, in fact, modified flattened stems called cladodes. Cladodes produce tiny flowers that are followed by small red fruit. However, only the foliage is generally required for most sugar work.

cladodes

1 Roll out some mid-green flower paste, leaving a thicker central ridge. Cut out the cladode using either a sharp scalpel or a ruscus cutter. Insert a moistened 28- or 26-gauge wire depending upon the size of the leaf.

2 Vein the leaf using either a fresh ruscus leaf or a dried sweetcorn husk. If you decide to use a fresh leaf, bear in mind that the veins are very subtle and so you will need to apply plenty of pressure. Then pinch the leaf at both the base and tip. Repeat this process to make the required number of leaves.

materials

Mid-green flower paste (gum paste)
28-, 26- and 20-gauge green wire
Holly/ivy and dark green dusting powders (petal dust/blossom tint)
3/4 glaze
Nile green floristry tape

◆

equipment

Ruscus cutter [CC] or sharp scalpel
Fresh ruscus leaf or a dried sweetcorn husk

colouring

3 Dust heavily with dark green and holly/ivy dusting powders. Once dry, dip into a 3/4 glaze.

4 Tape the cladodes together into groups of two and three. Tape them on to a 20-gauge green wire, starting with one set of leaves and then spiralling the others down the stem. (For the larger ruscus, the leaves are taped on individually.)
  Finally, coat the main stem with the two green dusting powders. Use the glaze to seal the coloured paste.

Green Man New Year Celebration

This unusual New Year's Eve cake features a green man, grape vine and flaming trumpet vine. The Green Man was originally a pagan symbol of natural law that has been incorporated into Christian Church ornament and architecture. The design created here depicts the oldest symbol of the green man and is perfect for New Year celebrations.

cake & decoration

20cm (8in) elliptical-shaped fruit cake
Apricot glaze
750g (1½lb) white almond paste (marzipan)
Clear alcohol (kirsch, white rum, cointreau etc)
750g (1½lb) champagne sugarpaste (rolled fondant)
Pastillage or mixture of sugarpaste and flower paste coloured pale green
White, holly/ivy and forest green dusting powders (petal dust/blossom tint)
Broad pale green ribbon for cake base
Gold lustre colour
Egg white

◆

equipment

20cm (8in) elliptical-shaped cake board
Medium egg mould
Dresden tool and ball tool
Grape vine leaf cutters [J]
Very large bramble type veiner
Florists' green staysoft or block of dry oasis
Non-slip mat and tilting turntable
Sponge (optional)
25cm (10in) elliptical-shaped bonsai tray
25cm (10in) rectangular bonsai dish
Green plastic separator

◆

flowers

3 stems of flaming trumpet vine (see p.110)
3 stems of grape vine leaves (see step 3)
5 stems of hop leaves (see p.21 of *Wild Flowers* in the 'Sugar Inspiration' series)

preparation

1 Put the cake on the board and brush with apricot glaze. Cover both the cake and edge of the board with almond paste and allow to dry. Brush the surface of the almond paste with alcohol and cover with champagne sugarpaste. Allow to dry. Attach a band of broad pale green ribbon to the base of the cake.

top design

2 Make a base for the head by lining an egg mould with pastillage, trimming the edge and allowing it to dry. Next, apply a thick layer of pastillage over the dried egg shape and hollow out two eye sockets half-way down the face using a ball tool. Build up the forehead and cheek bones by applying some more paste. (Do not worry about the joins as these can be covered with foliage.) Model a nose and mouth and attach to the face, using a dresden tool to blend the pastes together.

Roll two balls for the eyes and insert into the sockets. Indent the centre. Add lids to the bottom and top of each eye.

3 Roll out some flower paste and cut out two large, two medium and two small grapevine leaves. Soften the edges of each and then vein using the bramble type veiner. Attach the two medium leaves around the eyes and over the cheeks. Position the two large leaves over the forehead and add the two small leaves to either side of the mouth — try to blend the base of each leaf into the lips. Build up a heavy leaf stalk on to the base of the large leaf on the forehead.

4 Dust the whole head with a mixture of white, holly/ivy and forest green dusting powders. (Alternatively, dilute the colours with alcohol and hand paint the face to achieve more depth.) Allow the paste to dry before painting the eyes. Catch the leaves, nose and lips with some gold lustre colour.

5 Place the cake on a tilting turntable and attach the head with either royal icing or softened flower paste mixed with fresh egg white. If necessary, the head can be supported with a piece of sponge. Ensure that the paste is completely dry before removing the cake from the turntable.

assembly

6 Place a green plastic separator (in this case the lid from a spray can!) on top of the rectangular bonsai dish. Put a non-slip mat on top of the lid and then position the cake on the elliptical tray.

The flowers are inserted and arranged in staysoft behind the cake, and the leaves are simply placed around the base to fill the gap between the two bonsai dishes.

Flaming Trumpet Vine

(Pyrostegia venusta)

There are five species of *Pyrostegia*, and all are native to South America. The flaming trumpet vine is from Brazil and is the most popular and commonly cultivated of the species. The plant is usually grown as a climber, but it can also make an interesting display when used as ground cover.

materials

Small white seed-head stamens
Non-toxic hick-tack craft glue
28-, 26-, 24- and 20-gauge white wire
Pale melon, green and mid-holly/ivy
flower paste (gum paste)
Egg white
Tangerine, red, vine, primrose, lemon,
moss and forest green dusting powders
(petal dust/blossom tint)
½ glaze
Nile green floristry tape

equipment

Grooved board
Celstick
Round tip four-petalled
cutters – small and
medium [SC]
Sharp scissors
Dresden veining tool
Sharp scalpel
Black bryony leaf cutters
[TT653, 654]
Bittersweet veiner [GI]

flowers

1 Cut the tip off of one long seed-head stamen and glue this, together with two stamens, on to the end of a piece of 26-gauge wire. Allow to dry.

2 Form a ball of well-kneaded pale melon flower paste into a cone shape. Pinch out the base of the cone to create a pedestal shape. Place the flat side of the pedestal against the board and thin out the base using a celstick. Cut out the flower shape with the medium round tip, four-petalled cutter.

3 Soften the edges of the petal with the rounded end of a celstick and open up the throat using the pointed end of the tool.

4 Moisten the base of the stamens with fresh egg white and thread

7 Attach a tiny ball of green flower paste to the base of each flower and bud. Snip the ball into four sections using the pair of fine, sharp scissors.

colouring

8 Dust each bud and flower with tangerine-coloured dusting powder. Darken the throat of each flower and catch the tip of each bud with red dusting powder. Next, dust the calyx with a little vine green. Dust the tips of the stamens with primrose and lemon dusting powders.

leaves

9 The leaves pictured here have been made with some artistic licence! (The true leaves of this plant are more slender in shape.) To make them, roll

10 Dust the leaves with lemon, vine green, moss green, forest green and holly/ivy dusting powders. Dip the coloured paste into a ½ glaze.

11 Tape the leaves into sets of five and three using half width nile green tape. Tape the buds and flowers into tight clusters.

12 To tape a full stem of flaming trumpet vine you will need to make some tendrils. Twist some half width nile green floristry tape back on to itself, to create a long strand. Cut three tendrils and tape them on to the end of a piece of 24-gauge wire.

Finally, tape the various components on to a piece of 20-gauge wire. Every time you introduce a cluster of flowers or buds to the stem, remember to add a set of leaves.

them through the centre of the flower. Thin down the paste on the reverse of the flower to form a tapered back. Trim off the excess.

5 Use a sharp pair of scissors to split one of the petals into two sections. Vein each petal down the centre using the fine end of the dresden tool. Curl the tips of each petal back slightly.

buds

6 Attach a cone-shaped piece of paste over a moistened, hooked, 28- or 26-gauge white wire. Thin the base of the cone down on to the wire.

Divide the tip into four sections using a sharp scalpel. Give the bud a curved shape. You will need to make the buds in graduating sizes.

out some mid-holly/ivy flower paste, leaving a thick ridge for the wire. Cut out a leaf shape using a bryony leaf cutter. Insert a moistened 26-gauge wire into the paste. Soften the edges and vein the surface with the bittersweet leaf veiner. Repeat to make the leaves in sets of three and five.

Orchid Bee Frenzy

This cake features a very green combination of slipper orchids, caladium and jasmine foliage.
A frenzy of iridescent orchid bees makes an unusual and yet fitting side companion on the cake, which
would be suitable for a birthday or silver anniversary.

cake & decoration

25cm (10in) elliptical-shaped rich fruit cake
Apricot glaze
1.25kg (2½lb) white almond paste
(marzipan)
Clear alcohol (kirsch, white rum,
cointreau etc)
2kg (4lb) white sugarpaste (rolled fondant)
Small amount of royal icing
Green velvet ribbon to trim the edge of
the cake board
Non-toxic glue stick
Small amount of white flower paste
(gum paste)
Lime green ribbon
to trim the base of the cake
Small amount of cornflour (cornstarch)
Small amount of gildesol
Black, vine green, holly/ivy and forest green
dusting powders (petal dust/blossom tint)
Iridescent blue and pale green dusting
powders (petal dust/blossom tint)

◆

equipment

Sugarpaste smoothers
36cm (14in) elliptical-shaped cake board
Small oval acrylic board [HP]
Bumble-bee mould/cutter [HH]
Sharp scalpel
Piping bag fitted with a no.1 piping
tube (tip)
Fine paintbrushes
Florists' green staysoft or a small block
of dry oasis

◆

flowers

Green Orchid Arrangement (see p.114)

preparation

1 Brush the cake with warmed apricot glaze and cover with white almond paste. Leave to dry overnight. Moisten with clear alcohol and then cover with white sugarpaste, using smoothers to create a smooth finish.

Place a pad of sugarpaste in the palm of your hand and smooth the surface and edges, using fairly fast, smooth movements. Always smooth away from the surface, otherwise the two pieces of paste will stick together.

2 Cover the board with sugarpaste and put the cake on top. Use the smoothers to create a neat join between the base of the cake and the board.

Apply a small amount of royal icing to the back of the cake and attach a band of lime green ribbon.

orchid bees

3 Roll out a small amount of well-kneaded flower paste, leaving the centre slightly thicker. Dust the surface with cornflour and cut out the bee using the mould/cutter. Scrub the cutter against the board to get a clean cut.

Lift the cutter up and rub your thumb over the edge. Press down with your thumb to pick up the full veining from the mould. Use a damp finger to remove the paste – avoid using anything too sharp as this will damage the cutter. Make 20–22 orchid bees.

4 Using a sharp scalpel, split the wings and trim any excess paste away. Pull the top half of each wing over the bottom half. Paint the body of each bee with black dusting powder diluted with a small amount of clear alcohol and allow to dry.

Dust over the bottom half of the body and at the tip of the head with a mixture of the iridescent dusts. Apply a tiny amount of gildesol to the bottom half of the bees' bodies and then overdust with the iridescent dust (this will create a stronger colour). Dust the bees' wings lightly with the iridescent colour too.

Using a small amount of royal icing, attach the orchid bees to the sides of the cake. Then, to complete the side design, dilute a mixture of forest, vine green and holly/ivy powders with clear alcohol and use a fine paintbrush to add trailing dots behind each bee. Add a single dot at intervals between the insects. Alternatively, you could pipe the dots using green royal icing and a piping bag fitted with a no.1 tube.

5 Using the non-toxic glue stick, attach the green velvet ribbon to the edge of the board. Dust the surface of the board lightly with pale green, iridescent dusting powder.

assembly

6 Glue a piece of staysoft to the acrylic oval board and allow to dry. Arrange the flowers and foliage as described on page 114. Place the arrangement on top of the cake and re-adjust as necessary.

Use a medium-sized dusting brush to add vine green dusting powder around the base of the arrangement and out towards the edges of the cake. This will help to blend the arrangement.

Green Orchid Arrangement

Green has always been my favourite colour and, when I think of orchids, it is always this green and white slipper orchid that springs to mind. Here, I have combined them with caladium and jasmine foliage to create a fresh and green arrangement. I have used only two orchids in the display, which might seem strange to experienced sugarcrafters, florists and flower arrangers, but with new styles developing constantly, this is now an accepted practice.

flowers

2 slipper orchids and 9 orchid leaves
(see p.116)
5 stems of jasmine with buds (see p.38 of
Floral Wedding Cakes & Sprays)
5 caladium leaves (see p.97)

◆

equipment

Florists' green staysoft or a small block
of dry oasis
Small oval acrylic board [HP]
Non-toxic high-tack craft glue
Wire cutters
Fine-nosed pliers

preparation

1 Fix a ball of florists' staysoft on to the acrylic board using a small amount of non-toxic high-tack glue. Press the ball on to the board to form a domed shape. Allow the glue to dry completely before you start to arrange the flowers into the staysoft.

assembly

2 Cut both of the orchid stems to the required length and make a small, open hook in the end of each of the stems. The stems will then need to be arranged into the staysoft; the hook on the end of the wire will prevent the flowers from moving around once they are set in position.

3 Next, add the orchid foliage to create a fan shape in the arrangement. Bend a hook in the end of the jasmine stems and then position them evenly around the spray, so that you end up with a finished piece that is well balanced.

4 Bend a hook into the end of each of the caladium wire stems and then insert them into the staysoft. This should fill the recess of the flower arrangement.

5 Finally, stand back from the orchid display so that you can check to see if any of the flowers or foliage are in need of re-positioning. Some of the stems may need gently relaxing, so that they hang more naturally.

Slipper Orchid
(Paphiopedilum)

Paphiopedilum orchids are my favourite group of the orchid family.
Sadly, all slipper orchids growing in the wild today are considered to be
endangered species and, despite the fact that they are listed, the best protected
plants are those growing in botanical gardens and private collections.
Paphiopedilum orchids are native to southern China, India, Burma, Malaysia,
Borneo, the Philippines and New Guinea. The slipper-like lip of the
orchid is used to trick insects into pollinating the flower; the only
exit from the slipper is at the back and up past the
stamens – thus forcing the insect to rub its
back against the stamens. Slipper orchids
are wonderfully fun and very stylish
flowers to use in bouquets and in
arrangements on cakes.

materials

White, pale green and mid-holly/ivy
flower paste (gum paste)
Egg white
26-, 24-, 22-, 20- and 18-gauge
white wire
Vine green, moss green, holly/ivy,
forest green, primrose and
aubergine dusting powders
(petal dust/blossom tint)
Isopropyl alcohol
Full and ¹/₂ glaze
Confectioners' varnish
Nile green floristry tape

◆

equipment

Slipper orchid templates
(see p.157)
Card or thin plastic
Sharp scalpel
Foam pad
Large celstick or large ball tool
Plain edge cutting wheel [PME]
Cocktail stick (toothpick)
or scriber
Slipper orchid veiner set [GI]
Dresden veining tool

slipper (labellum)

1 The slipper is the most difficult part of this flower – it requires a lot of time both to make and dry. Begin by tracing out the slipper template on to a piece of card or thin plastic. (A margarine tub, plastic milk carton or sheet of plastic from a craft shop are all suitable mediums.)

Roll out a large piece of well-kneaded white flower paste (not too thinly), leaving the paste slightly thicker at the centre. Place the slipper template shape on top of the paste and cut out the shape using a sharp scalpel.

2 Put the slipper shape on a pad and soften the edges, especially the upper edges, with the rounded end of a large celstick. Hollow out the base on either side of the thick ridge with either the celstick or a large ball tool.

3 Moisten one side of the bottom curved edge of the slipper. Use egg white for this, rather than gum glue, edible glue or gum arabic.

4 Begin to form the slipper shape. To do this, you will need to overlap the two bottom curved edges of the flower paste. Use the rounded end of a large celstick to help achieve the shape of the slipper throat. As you start to form the throat, press the join in the petal firmly with your thumb. Blend the join further by pressing the rounded end of the celstick against it.

5 Place the slipper on the pad and continue to cup and hollow out the shape using the rounded end of the celpick. At the top of the slipper, carefully curl the top cut edges in towards each other. Use the plain edge cutting wheel to add a central vein to the front of the slipper orchid.

6 Bend a hook in the end of a 20-gauge wire. Cover the wire with some white flower paste that has been softened and mixed with fresh egg white. Pull the hooked wire through the centre and at an angle. Then squeeze the various parts together slightly, so that they merge completely. Allow to dry.

colouring

7 Dust the slipper heavily with vine green dusting powder. Add depth to the base of the slipper by applying the holly/ivy and forest green powders. Add a touch of aubergine to the edge of the slipper mouth.

8 Dilute some of the darker greens with a dash of isopropyl alcohol. Use the mixture to paint some fine veins on to the surface of the slipper, pulling the strokes out from the main central vein.

Allow the paste to dry before dipping into a full glaze. Pour out the excess glaze from the slipper and repeat until you have the desired finish. Leave aside to dry.

column

9 The column and stamen used in this version is a much simpler structure than that found in the real flower. First, roll a ball of well-kneaded white flower paste into a cone shape. Flatten out the base of the cone and pinch one part into a point.

Next, use a sharp scalpel to mark out a central vein. Try to pull the side that is opposite the point into a V-shape (the finished column should resemble that of a heart).

Insert some softened flower paste into the dried slipper and attach the column. Dust with vine and holly/ivy dusting powders and catch the edges with a tiny amount of aubergine. Using a cocktail stick or scriber, add a hole to the centre of the column. A drop of confectioners' varnish can be added to suggest nectar.

lateral petals (wing petals)

10 Roll out some white flower paste, leaving a thick ridge at the centre for a wire. Use either the flat side of one of the double-sided petal veiners

(or a template from page 157) with a sharp scalpel to cut out the petal shape. Insert a moistened 26-gauge wire into the thick ridge of the paste and pinch the base of the petal to secure it.

11 Position the paste on a pad and soften the edges. Vein the surface using the double-sided petal veiner. (Alternatively, you can add freehand veins with the fine end of the dresden tool.) Turn the petal over and mark a strong, central vein – this should form a ridge on the reverse side of the petal. Allow the paste to firm up into a gentle curve. Repeat this process to make two wing petals.

dorsal sepal

12 Roll out some more white flower paste. Then, using either the flat side of the dorsal veiner or the template from page 157 and a sharp scalpel, cut out the basic shape. Insert a piece of 26-gauge white wire into the thick ridge and pinch the base into a sharp point.

Soften the edges of the paste and then vein the surface using either the double-sided veiner or the dresden tool. (The veins should curve out from the base and back in again at the tip). Curl back the edges at the base of the sepal. Leave the paste aside to firm up a little, before colouring.

base sepal

13 Repeat the process described to make the base sepal. However, you will need to use either the base sepal template or the double-sided veiner, to obtain the correct shape. Leave the paste to dry, as before.

colouring & assembly

14 Mix together holly/ivy, vine green and forest green dusting powders, and dilute with a small amount of isopropyl alcohol. Paint a series of fine lines on to the dorsal and base sepals – but remember that the lines on the dorsal should be slightly bolder. Add some lines to the back of each sepal.

The wing petals should have some tiny pimples left by the veiner. Paint over each of the pimples with a small amount of colour and then add some fine veins to the bottom half of each petal.

15 Dust the base and the tip of the dorsal sepal and base sepal with vine green dusting powder. Add a little holly/ivy colour for further depth. Dust the wing petals with vine green powder and then dust the upper half of each petal with holly/ivy and a touch of moss green.

16 Tape a couple of 18-gauge wires alongside the main stem using half width nile green floristry tape. Attach the wing petals to either side of the slipper and then add the dorsal and base sepals.

ovary & bract

17 Attach a sausage of pale green flower paste to the back of the flower. Thin out either end of the sausage shape to make it look slightly padded at the centre. Use a pair of fine-angled tweezers to create several long ridges over the surface of the ovary, from the top to the bottom. Next, gently curve the stem. The ovary and stem should then be dusted with holly/ivy and vine green powders. For further effect, add a touch of aubergine to the back of the flower.

18 Roll out pale green flower paste and cut out the bract shape using the template from page 157. Soften and vein the bract shape and attach it to the base of the ovary. Dust the paste as for the ovary.

leaves

19 Roll out some mid-holly/ivy flower paste, not too thinly, leaving a thick ridge for the wire. Cut out the leaf shape freehand using the leaf template on page 157 and a sharp scalpel. Alternatively, you could use the plain edge cutting wheel.

Insert a moistened 24-, 22- or 20-gauge wire (depending upon the size of the leaf) into the thick ridge. Position the paste on a pad and soften the edges. Vein the centre of the leaf strongly using the fine end of the dresden tool. Turn the shape over against the pad and hollow out the underside of the leaf using the rounded end of the celpick. Pinch the leaf firmly between your finger and thumb. Repeat this process to make leaves of several sizes.

colouring

20 Mix forest green and holly/ivy dusting powder with isopropyl alcohol. Paint a series of veins on to each leaf. Allow the surface to dry before painting lots of spots over the top of the leaf. (The dots should only be added to the upper surface of the leaf.) Dust with holly/ivy and forest green dusting powders. Finally, tinge the base and tip of each leaf with aubergine dusting powders before dipping into a ½ glaze.

Chinese Whispers

Rice paper, cocoa butter and dusting powders have been used to create the stylized bird design on this attractive birthday cake. Rice paper is a very useful, yet undervalued and under-used material: it is very good for the cake decorator with limited time and little patience as it requires no drying time! When rice paper is combined with cocoa butter, you can achieve some very subtle paint effects. However, be very careful not to get the paper too moist as this can cause it to curl or even dissolve.

cake & decoration

20cm (8in) long, octagonal-shaped rich fruit cake
Apricot glaze
750g (1½lb) white almond paste (marzipan)
Clear alcohol (kirsch, white rum, cointreau etc)
1kg (2lb) pink sugarpaste (rolled fondant)
Small amount of royal icing or softened sugarpaste (rolled fondant)
Fine magenta ribbon to trim the cake
15mm (½in) magenta ribbon to trim the edge of the cake board
Non-toxic glue stick
Small amount of cocoa butter
African violet, holly/ivy, vine green, forest green, deep purple, dark green, plum, white, primrose, lemon, nutkin brown and brown dusting powders
(petal dust/blossom tint)
Rice paper

◆

equipment

Sugarpaste smoothers
30cm (12in) long octagonal cake board
Bird and flower templates (see p.158)
Tracing or greaseproof paper
Scriber
Mug and saucer with hot water
Sharp scalpel
Fine and medium paintbrushes
Soft brush
Fine sharp scissors

◆

flowers

1 camellia (see p.123)

preparation

1 Brush the fruit cake with apricot glaze and cover with white almond paste. Allow the cake to dry for a few hours – overnight if possible.

Moisten the surface of the almond paste with clear alcohol and cover with pink sugarpaste. Use the smoothers and the sugarpaste pad technique to produce a flawless, smooth finish to the surface.

2 Cover the cake board with sugarpaste and place the cake on top, making sure that there is a neat join between the base of the cake and the board. Allow to dry.

3 Attach a band of fine magenta ribbon and a small bow to the base of the cake using a small amount of royal icing or some softened sugarpaste. Glue a length of magenta ribbon to the edge of the board using the non-toxic glue stick. Leave the cake aside to dry.

cake top design

4 Trace the flower and bird design on to tracing or greaseproof paper. Scribe the design through the paper on to the surface of the cake.

Melt a small amount of cocoa butter on a saucer above a mug filled with just boiled water. In order to achieve a soft, opaque finish to the coloured cocoa butter, mix in some white dusting powder.

Add your chosen colour. The flowers behind the bird are painted directly on to the surface of the sugarpaste, and you can choose whether to paint the flowers, branch or leaves first. If you are aiming to use several colours, or to achieve a depth of colour on one piece, it is important to allow the first layer of cocoa butter to set slightly before applying the next coat. On this cake I have used vine green, holly/ivy and forest green dusting powders (mixed with the butter) for the leaves. The flowers are painted with plum and white to various degrees, and the stamens are a mixture of primrose and lemon, topped with brown anthers.

When the design has set, etch away with a scalpel some of the cocoa butter to create veins in the petals and leaves. Use a soft brush to remove the excess pieces of cocoa butter. Add a small detail design to the cake board.

5 Trace the bird designs (page 158) on to rice paper using a sharp pencil and cut out the various shapes. To create the 3-D découpage effect, soften

some sugarpaste with clear alcohol to form a consistency similar to that of royal icing. (Avoid making the mixture too wet as the rice paper will dissolve and disintegrate). Layer the various sections on top of one another with pads of softened paste between each.

6 Paint in the design using cocoa butter and dusting powder. To create a stronger image, outline each section with deep purple and dark green dusting powders. Ideally, each layer should be painted so that when viewed from the side, you do not see any white patchy areas. However, there is little point in adding fine detail to areas that are not going to be seen, so only give these layers a quick coat or simply push the paintbrush under each layer when using the different colours.

As with the painted flowers, start each section with fairly pale colours. Allow the first layer to set slightly before increasing the colour intensity and adding further, more intricate detail to the paintwork.

7 When the bird is complete, attach it to the cake with a small amount of softened sugarpaste. Use a medium-sized brush and some white dusting powder, mixed with a small amount of plum, to add colour around the flowers and bird. Finally, position the single camellia at the base of the cake.

Camellia

Camellias have been intensively cultivated by the Chinese and Japanese
for so long that there are numerous Asiatic cultivars. The flower pictured is a single variety,
based on *C. japonica* and *C. sasanqua*, but there are also semi-double and double-flowered
forms. Tea-seed oil is derived from *C. sasanqua* and is used for textile purposes in the silk
industry and also in the production of soap. Tsubaki oil is obtained
from *C. japonica* and can be used as a hair oil.

materials

26-, 24- and 20-gauge white wire
Nile green floristry tape
Small white seed-head stamens
Non-toxic high-tack craft glue
White, pale pink, pale and mid-holly/ivy
flower paste (gum paste)
Lemon, primrose, plum, white,
forest green, holly/ivy, vine green and
aubergine dusting powders
(petal dust/blossom tint)
Deep magenta craft dust (optional)
Egg white
³/₄ glaze

◆

equipment

Fine-nosed pliers and wire cutters
Small sharp scissors
Fine-angled tweezers
Large rose petal cutters [TT550, 551]
Small rose petal cutters
[277, 278, 279, 280]
Grooved board (optional)
Ceramic silk veining tool
Large celstick
Plain edge cutting wheel [PME]
Dresden veining tool
Foam pad
Camellia leaf veiners [GI]
Ball tool (optional)

stamens

1 Bend a very round, open hook in the end of a 24-gauge wire. Hold the hooked end with some fine-nosed pliers and bend to form a ski-stick shape. Tape on to a 20-gauge wire using half width nile green floristry tape.

2 Glue together small groups of tiny, white seed-head stamens using some non-toxic glue. Start glueing at the centre of each small group, squeezing the glue into the stamen strands to form a neat finish. Leave some length unglued at both ends of the stamens. Put aside to firm and then cut in half.

Trim off the excess stamen to create the required length. You will need to use between three quarters and a full bunch of stamens per flower. Again using a tiny amount of glue, attach the small groups of stamens around the edge of the hooked wire.

Squeeze the stamens firmly into position, in order to ensure that they stick properly. Once dry, bend the tips of the stamens a little using a pair of tweezers. Dust the tips of the stamens with a mixture of primrose and lemon dusting powders.

3 At the centre of the stamens there is a pistil that is divided into three sections. Twist three pieces of half width nile green tape into three strands and then tape them together, leaving the tips curled at the top. Glue into the centre of the stamens and allow to dry. Coat with vine green dusting powder.

petals

4 Squeeze the largest rose petal cutter to form a slightly narrowed shape. Roll out some pale pink flower paste, leaving the centre slightly thicker than

the sides. Alternatively, you may prefer to use a grooved board.

Cut out a rose petal shape with a cutting wheel. Then insert a moistened, hooked 26-gauge white wire into the base of the petal. Using a pair of small, sharp scissors, cut out a curved V-shape from the top of the petal to create a heart shape.

5 Place the petal back against the board and vein the surface gently on both sides with the ceramic silk veining tool. (You will need to vein the petal in a fan formation.)

Frill the edges very slightly with the silk veining tool, but remember that camellias are generally not very frilly, so avoid excessive use. Pinch the petal gently down the centre to create a central vein. Repeat to make five petals. Allow to firm slightly before adding dusting powder.

colouring & assembly

6 Dust each petal using plum dusting powder or deep magenta craft dust, mixed with a small amount of white. (Magenta produces a stronger pink colour.) Begin by working in from the edges of each petal, on both the back and front. Dust up from the bottom of each petal, leaving some of the base colour showing through.

7 Tape the five petals tightly around the stamens, positioning two of the petals directly opposite one another. If the paste is still slightly wet, you should be able to curl the edges of each petal to produce a more relaxed flower shape.

Hang the flower upside down until it is firm enough to hold its shape without the wires becoming exposed.

calyx

8 Roll out some pale holly/ivy flower paste and cut out five small rose petal shapes using a small rose petal cutter. Soften the edges and then cup each petal with the rounded end of the large celstick.

Moisten the base of each sepal and then attach two sepals opposite one another on the back of the flower, at the base. Attach the remaining three sepals and pinch the base of each to make the calyx fit into place. Dust with vine green and holly/ivy dusting powders.

buds

9 Roll a ball of white flower paste. Insert a hooked, moistened 20-gauge wire into the base and pinch the paste firmly around the wire to secure it in place. Allow to dry.

10 Roll out some more of the pink paste and cut out five small rose petal shapes. (The number and size will depend upon the size of the dried paste that forms the centre for the bud.) Vein and frill the petal in the same way as you did for the flower. Moisten each petal and place around the bud, scrunching each to create a natural shape.

Dust with plum or deep magenta craft dust (or your chosen colour) mixed with white dusting powder. Then, attach a calyx using slightly smaller rose petal cutters than those used for the flower. Dust as before. Thicken the stem using nile green floristry tape.

leaves

11 Roll out some mid-holly/ivy-coloured flower paste on to a grooved board. Alternatively, roll out the paste using a small rolling pin but leave the centre of the paste slightly thicker.

Cut out a leaf shape with the large end of the plain edge cutting wheel. Moisten and insert a 26- or 24-gauge

wire (depending on the size of the leaf) into the thick ridge.

12 Using the broad end of the dresden veining tool to work the edges of the leaf, pull out small points around the leaf shape. You will need to press firmly against the paste on to the board, and drag the tool slightly, in order to create the desired effect. Position the leaf on a pad and soften the edges gently but do not frill it.

13 Put the leaf into one of the camellia leaf veiners and press firmly to create definite veining on the leaf. Pinch the leaf along the stem, from the base to the tip.

Hollow out the undersides of some of the larger leaves using a ball tool or the round end of the celstick, taking care not to remove too much of the veining. Allow the camellia leaves to firm up a little but do not allow them to dry totally before dusting.

14 Dust the backs and edges of each leaf with vine green. Overdust the surface heavily with forest green and a touch of aubergine and holly/ivy in places. Dip the leaves into a ³/₄ glaze and allow to dry.

Use a sharp scalpel blade to create a paler, central vein by etching through the glaze and colour, helping to reveal the paler sugar colour beneath.

Cattleya Orchid Wedding Cake

Silver and lilac is an increasingly popular, modern choice of colours for brides and bridesmaids. This cake is ideal for such a wedding, because of its contemporary feel. Bold silver foliage and chillies combine with delicate lilac cattleya orchids to create a stunning display that is both decorative and vibrant. Space is very important when trying to create a modern effect, here I have used a slender silver candle holder to display some of the flowers to create artistic space.

cake & decoration

20cm (8in) teardrop-shaped rich fruit cake
and 30cm (12in) oval-shaped rich fruit cake
Apricot glaze
2kg (4lb) white almond paste (marzipan)
Clear alcohol (kirsch, white rum,
cointreau etc)
3kg (6lb) white sugarpaste
(rolled fondant)
Small amount of royal icing
Silver ribbon to trim the base of the cake
and cake board
Lilac ribbon to trim the cake board
Non-toxic glue stick
Lilac organza-type ribbon, made into
wired loops to use in the sprays

◆

equipment

Sugarpaste smoothers
38cm (15in) oval-shaped cake board
Scrolled silver candle holder
Silver spray paint
Fine-nosed pliers and wire cutters
White floristry tape
Cake pick
Florists' green staysoft or a small block of
dry oasis

◆

flowers

2 cattleya orchids (see p.128)
7 philodendron leaves (see p.25)
18 Christmas chilli peppers (see p.144)

preparation

1 Brush both cakes with apricot glaze and cover the surfaces with almond paste, then leave them aside to dry. Turn the teardrop-shaped cake on to its side and cover the base with a layer of almond paste. Moisten the surface of the almond paste with clear alcohol and cover with white sugarpaste.

Cover the cake board with sugarpaste and transfer the base cake on top. Place the small teardrop-shaped cake on top of the oval-shaped cake as pictured.

2 Attach a band of silver ribbon to the base of both of the cakes using a small amount of royal icing or softened sugarpaste. Attach a band of lilac ribbon, followed by silver ribbon, to the edge of the board using the non-toxic glue stick.

3 Position the candle holder on top of the base tier. Fill the cup of the holder with a small amount of staysoft to help hold the orchid spray. Spray the chillies and philodendron leaves with silver paint and leave to dry.

assembly

4 Wire up two small sprays using white floristry tape and add an orchid to each. Insert the smaller spray into the staysoft in the candle holder, then add a trailing band of ribbon. Insert the larger flower spray into the cake pick and insert this into the base cake. Add a small set of silver leaves to the base of the cake to complete the design.

Cattleya Orchid

Cattleya orchids, sometimes known as 'chocolate box' orchids,
are the most flamboyant and frilly members of the orchid family. There
are approximately 60 species of cattleya orchid, with most plants originating from
the rainforests of South America. I was taught this orchid in one of my very first
classes, when I was 15 years old, so it brings back memories of my first
introduction to wired sugar flowers. Cattleya orchids are used to a much
greater extent in bridal bouquets and corsages in America, Australia
and South Africa than they are in Great Britain. The colour
range is vast, mainly due to the cross-hybridization
between the cattleya and the laelia orchid.

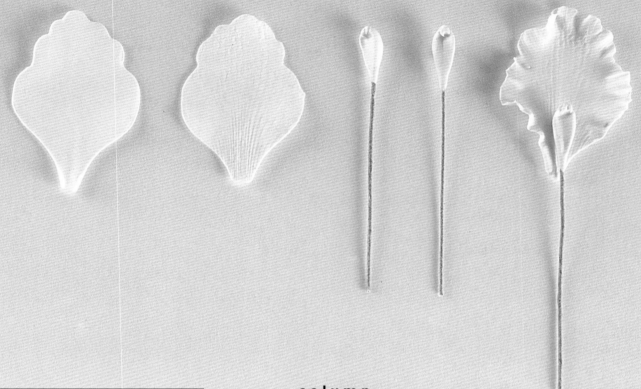

materials

White flower paste (gum paste)
26-, 24- and 20-gauge white wire
Egg white
African violet, primrose, lemon, plum,
vine and foliage green dusting powders
(petal dust/blossom tint)
Isopropyl alcohol
Nile green floristry tape

◆

equipment

Celstick
Sharp scalpel
Cattleya orchid cutters [J]
Amaryllis petal veiner [GI]
Dresden veining tool
Ceramic silk veining tool [HP]
Sharp scissors
Fine and large paintbrushes
Small rolling pin

column

1 Form a ball of well-kneaded, white flower paste into a teardrop shape. Moisten the end of a 20-gauge white wire with fresh egg white and insert it into the fine end of the teardrop. Use the rounded end of a celstick to hollow out the upper part of the column, pinching the back to form a slight ridge. To make the anther cap, add a tiny ball of paste to the front of the column on the underside, and use a sharp scalpel to divide it into two. Leave aside to dry.

throat (labellum)

2 Roll out some white flower paste to a fleshy thickness, leaving a ridge at the centre to give support. Cut out the throat shape using the throat cutter from the orchid set. Vein the petal heavily using the amaryllis veiner.

3 Double frill the edges of the petal using the broad end of the dresden tool. Soften them by overfrilling with the ceramic silk veining tool. Use a sharp pair of scissors to remove a small, V-shaped cut from the tip of the petal.

4 Apply a little fresh egg white to the base and sides of the petal. Put the dried column on top of the petal and then attach one side of the petal over the column. Next, overlap this edge with the other side of the petal. Curl back the edges slightly.

There should be some space between the column and the throat petal. If this is not the case, try opening the throat with the pointed end of a paintbrush. Allow the paste to dry.

colouring

5 Dust the very heart of the throat with a mixture of primrose and lemon dusting powders, taking care not to get the yellow colouring on the column itself. Dust the edges of the petal heavily with a mixture of African violet, plum and a small amount of white. Bring some of the colour on to the central part of the lip too.

6 Dilute some of the African violet dusting powder with isopropyl alcohol. Use a fine paintbrush to add some detail markings, extending from

the centre of the throat. With a larger brush, paint in from the edge of the petal, so that a bolder colour appears at the tip of the throat. Leave the paste aside to dry.

wing petals (lateral petals)

7 Roll out some white flower paste, leaving a thick ridge along the centre for inserting the wire. Cut out a wing petal shape using one of the two wing petal cutters in the set.

8 Insert a moistened 24-gauge white wire into the ridge of the petal, holding the paste firmly between your finger and thumb to prevent the wire from piercing through the surface.

Vein the petal using the double-sided amaryllis petal veiner. Frill the edges gently with the silk veining tool. Finally, pinch a subtle ridge down the centre of the upper side of the petal.

Repeat this procedure to make a left- and right-hand petal. The sugarpaste pieces should be left aside for a short while, so that they firm up with a gentle, graceful curve.

dorsal & lateral sepals

9 Roll out some more white flower paste with a small rolling pin, leaving a thick ridge at the centre. Cut out a sepal shape and insert a moistened 26-gauge wire into the thick ridge. Place the sepal on a pad and soften the edges gently. Pinch the base and the tip of the petal to create a slight central vein along the shape. Use this technique to make a total of three sepals.

Dry one petal in a curved position to form the dorsal sepal, with the other two curving back to represent the lateral sepals.

colouring & assembly

10 Dust the tips and the base of each flower petal using a mixture of African violet, plum and white dusting powders on a paintbrush.

11 Tape the two wing petals on to either side of the throat petal using half width nile green floristry tape. Add the dorsal and lateral sepals behind the wings and tape together tightly. If your petals are still slightly soft, you will be able to re-shape the flower to create a relaxed finish. Try to keep the throat petal pointed down at the heart of the flower.

Finally, dust the back of the flower at the base with a mixture of foliage green and vine green dusting powders.

note

The leaves of this plant are very large and are not usually used on cakes.

Ladder Fern
(Nephrolepsis)

This fern makes a very good partner to many members of the orchid family
and often the two are grown side by side. The only problem with this sugar version is that the fronds
are very fragile – it is therefore a good idea to wire them into the sprays before they have had
a chance to dry fully. Despite their fragility, these ferns are quick and quite easy to make
and they are perfect for filling out bouquets.

materials

Mid-holly/ivy flower paste (gum paste)
22-gauge wire
Egg white
Vine green, foliage green
and dark green dusting powders
(petal dust/blossom tint)
¼ glaze

◆

equipment

Grooved board
Rolling pin
Sword fern cutter [J]
Foam pad
Dresden veining tool
Nile green floristry tape
Fine-angled tweezers

fern frond

1 Roll out a large piece of green paste, but be careful not to make it too thin. Cut out the frond shape using the sword fern cutter. (You will find it easier to position the paste on top of the cutter and then roll the rolling pin over the top to obtain a cleaner cut.)

2 Remove the paste from the cutter and place it back on the board. Double frill both edges of each 'leaf' using the broad end of the dresden tool. Place the frond on a pad and draw a central vein on each of the 'leaves' using the fine end of the dresden tool.

3 Tape over a length of 22-gauge wire with some quarter width nile green floristry tape. Paint the wire with fresh egg white.
  Place the moistened wire down the centre of the fern, pressing firmly to ensure that it is secure. Quickly flip the leaf over and then pinch either side of the ridge with fine-angled tweezers. This will help to secure the wire and the leaf together. Turn the leaf back over and pinch the tips of each section. Curl them a little to create the impression of movement.

colouring

4 Dust the fern with a touch of dark green, then overdust the surface with plenty of vine green, and a little foliage green dusting powders. Bear in mind that younger ferns tend to be quite bright in colour, while older ferns are often darker.
  Dip the flower paste into a ¼ glaze. Shake off the excess glaze and leave aside to dry.

131

Peruvian Party Cake

This pretty pink cake would be suitable for a small birthday celebration. The flowers painted on to the cake have been created using coloured cocoa painting techniques, which help to give a soft, delicate finish. This design complements the vibrant pinks, yellows and whites of the sugar flower sprays and gives the whole display a sense of unity and style.

cake & decoration

15cm (6in) heart-shaped rich fruit cake
Apricot glaze
350g (12oz) white almond paste (marzipan)
Clear alcohol (kirsch, white rum,
cointreau etc)
500g (1lb) pale pink sugarpaste
(rolled fondant)
Small amount of cocoa butter
Plum, holly/ivy, forest green, lemon, white
and primrose dusting powders
(petal dust/blossom tint)
Fine, willow, colonial rose
and magenta ribbon
Small amount of royal icing
Magenta ribbon to trim the edge of
the cake board
Non-toxic glue stick

◆

equipment

Sugarpaste smoothers
20cm (8in) heart-shaped cake board
Mug of boiling water and saucer
Fine and medium paintbrushes
Cake design template (see p.157)
Sharp scalpel
Cake pick [W]

◆

flowers

Peruvian Party Spray (see p.134) plus
a small corsage and bower of beauty flower
(see p.10) to sit at the base
of the cake

preparation

1 Brush the cake with apricot glaze and cover with almond paste. Allow to dry. Moisten the cake with clear alcohol and cover with a layer of pale pink sugarpaste, using sugarpaste smoothers to achieve a good finish. Cover the cake board with sugarpaste and position the cake on top. Leave aside to dry.

side design

2 Melt a small amount of cocoa butter on a saucer above a mug of just boiled water. Mix small amounts of dusting powder with the melted cocoa butter on the side of the saucer; start by using white to paint in the basic shape of the blossoms.

Next, paint in the basic shape of the leaves using a base of holly/ivy and a touch of white dusting powder. Increase the depth of the green mixture with a touch of forest green and then shade in and add detail to the leaves using a finer brush. Paint in the flower and leaf stems at the same time.

Using a plum mixture and fine brush, add small dotted flowers and some detailed veining on the flower petals. Paint the centre of each flower with a mixture of lemon and primrose. Allow to dry before adding a mixture of white and plum dusting powders around the design. Use a sharp scalpel to etch away fine veins from the flowers and leaves.

3 Tie several lengths of coloured, fine ribbon together; twist them evenly and then tie a knot in the end. Use a small amount of royal icing to attach the twisted ribbons to the base of the cake. Glue magenta ribbon to the board edge.

4 Wire up the Peruvian Party Spray as instructed on page 134. Insert the spray into the cake with a cake pick. Wire together a smaller spray of buds and leaves with a single bower of beauty flower, and position this on the board.

Peruvian Party Spray

This pretty spray features on the Peruvian Party Cake and uses a single alstroemeria (common name – Peruvian lily) as its focal flower. The strong magenta colouring of the flower has been carried through the spray with the magenta-striped cordyline (South Sea Island ti) leaves. A posy is a good choice for a novice flower maker as the shape is easy to achieve – this style of spray is also known as a tussie mussie.

flowers

1 alstroemeria, plus 4 bud stems with foliage (see p.136)
5 stems of bower of beauty
– various combinations of flowers, buds and leaves (see p.10)
Several South Sea Island ti leaves (see p.26)

◆

equipment

Fine-nosed pliers
Nile green floristry tape
Wire cutters
Posy pick [W]
Suitable container

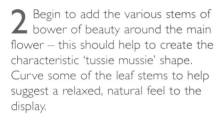

assembly

1 Start by taping the four alstroemeria bud stems around the focal alstroemeria flower, using the nile green floristry tape.

2 Begin to add the various stems of bower of beauty around the main flower – this should help to create the characteristic 'tussie mussie' shape. Curve some of the leaf stems to help suggest a relaxed, natural feel to the display.

3 Finally, add the South Sea Island ti leaves. The leaves should fill any vacant gaps and complete the overall shape. Trim the excess wire with wire cutters and neaten the handle of the spray with full width floristry tape.

4 Insert the handle of the spray into a plastic posy pick and then insert this into the container. Stand back from the arrangement and adjust any flowers as necessary.

Alstroemeria

Alstroemeria are often known by the common name of Peruvian lily, although the plant is also native to Chile and Brazil. Alstroemeria have become very popular as cut flowers as they can last a long time in water. However, they are poisonous and can cause skin irritation when handled for arrangements. There are numerous variations including pink, salmon, orange, red, lilac and white. Most flowers have numerous markings, although there are some hybrids without any marks at all.

materials

White, pink and nile green floristry tape
33-, 26-, 24-, 22- and 18-gauge
white wire
White or pale melon, pale and mid-
green flower paste (gum paste)
Dark green, holly/ivy, aubergine,
moss green, lemon and primrose dusting
powders (petal dust/blossom tint)
Deep magenta craft dust
Cyclamen liquid food colouring [SK]
½ glaze

equipment

Wire cutters
Nile green floristry tape
Fine-nosed pliers
Sharp scalpel
Fresh alstroemeria leaves or veiners [GI]
or Solomon seal leaf veiner
Foam pad
Fine paintbrush
Sharp scissors
Fine-angled tweezers
Plain edge cutting wheel [PME]

pistil

1 Twist a length of quarter width white or pink floristry tape back on to itself, stretching the tape as you go to form a thin strand. Cut three short lengths and tape them on to the end of a 33-gauge wire using quarter width floristry tape, before curling the tips. (Although the pistil is only visible in mature flowers, I add it to the sugar version for its interest value.)

stamens

2 Bend very small, closed hooks in the end of six short lengths of 33-gauge white wire. Attach small pieces of pale green flower paste to each of the hooked wires and smooth the paste between your finger and thumb, forming each anther into an oval shape. Press down on them to flatten. The stamens are quite fleshy when the flower first opens and then, as the pollen begins to develop, the anthers' size gradually reduces.

3 Tape the stamens around the pistil using quarter width nile green tape. Aim to make three of the stamens slightly shorter than the other three. Use a pair of fine-nosed pliers and a nipping action to curl the stamens and pistil into shape.

still slightly soft, as this enables a stronger colouring. It will also ensure that you can form a better shape to the flower.

Dust a streak of mixed primrose and lemon dusting powders on to the three narrow petals. Introduce some colour to the tips of each of the petals, making the two longer petals a touch bolder.

9 Paint some fine lines using a fine paintbrush and cyclamen liquid food colouring. Paint the lines at intervals over the surface of the three narrow petals but apply heavier markings to the two longer petals. Dust the very tips with a touch of moss green.

10 Dust the larger petals with your chosen colour and dust a heavy stripe of aubergine on the back of each. You can use the veins left by the veiner as a guide line.

11 Tape the two long petals together on to the set of stamens, with the stamens curving towards them. Add the smaller petal underneath the stamens.

Tape one of the broad petals behind the two long narrow petals, and then add the remaining two petals to either side of the flower. If the petals are still slightly wet you should be able to adjust the position of them to produce a natural finish.

4 Colour the anthers with a light coat of dark green dusting powder. The pistil and the filaments should be the same colour as the flower – in this case deep magenta.

narrow petals

5 There are three narrow petals; one of which is slightly shorter than the other two. Roll out some white or pale melon flower paste but leave a thick, central ridge. Using the flat part of one of the narrow petals, press firmly on to the paste to leave an outline. Cut out the petal shape using a sharp scalpel.

6 Insert a moistened piece of 26-gauge wire into the thick ridge. Place the petal on a pad and soften the edges. Vein the petal using the veiner as a template. Remove the petal from the veiner and pinch the tip into a sharp point (the tip should be pinched from the front to the back). Repeat to make one narrow, and two large, petals.

broad petals

7 Thinly roll out some white or pale melon flower paste, leaving a thick ridge. Use the flat side of the veiner as a template again and cut out the petal. Soften the edges and vein the paste using the two sides of the broad veiner. The edges of alstroemeria are actually very delicately serrated around the edge, although this can look strange when re-created in sugar.

Repeat to make three petals, pinching the tips from the back of each petal into a sharp point.

colouring & assembly

8 It is better to dust and tape the flower together while the petals are

ovary

12 Attach a ball of mid-green flower paste to the base of the flower and divide it into three sections using a

upside down! It is this twist at the base that makes the leaves appear as though they are the correct way up.

Roll out a long piece of mid-green flower paste but leave a thick ridge down the middle. Use the cutting wheel to cut out a long, pointed leaf shape from the paste.

16 Vein the leaf by using two fresh leaves together or a double-sided veiner. Soften the edges of the leaf and then twist the base. Pinch the tip of the leaf and allow to firm up a little before dusting and glazing.

17 Dust with dark green, holly/ivy and moss green dusting powders. Bear in mind that the backs of the leaves should be very pale in colour. Dust the tips with a touch of aubergine before dipping the paste into a ¹/₂ glaze.

assembly

18 Tape a couple of leaves behind each bud and flower. Tape the two together into small, individual groups. Add leaves each time you join several components together.

Attach the groups together on to several pieces of 18-gauge wire, using half width nile green floristry tape. Remember to add a ring of larger leaves to conceal the joins between each group of stems.

---

sharp scalpel. Pinch a ridge down the centre of each section using your finger and thumb.

Next, dust the ovary with dark green and moss green dusting powders. Carefully paint over the surface with a ¹/₂ glaze and allow to dry.

buds

13 Bend a hook in the end of a 24- or 22-gauge wire. (The gauge will depend upon the size of the bud you are planning to make.) Roll a ball of well-kneaded white or pale melon flower paste into a chubby cone shape and insert a moistened wire into the fine

end. Roll the tip of the bud to form a slight point. Divide the bud into three sections using a sharp scalpel.

14 Create veins and a ridge on the surface of the bud by using a pair of fine-angled tweezers. To give the largest buds the impression of petals that are beginning to open, simply cut the three sections at the tip with scissors. Pinch each point into a sharp point and add a smaller version of the ovary used on the back of the flower. The buds should be made in various sizes.

Dust the smaller buds with moss green and dark green dusting powders. Gradually introduce some of the flower colour – as the buds increase in size, the flower colour should increase and the amount of green should decrease. Finally, add some aubergine to the centre of each ridge on the bud.

leaves

15 You will need to make some small leaves to tape behind the buds and flowers and then a ring of larger leaves. It is best to have a real flower stem at this stage for ease of reference – you will find that the leaves have a distinct twist at the base, and are in fact attached to the stem

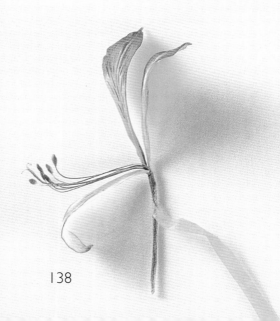

Fish-tail Fern

I came across this unusual fern in my local florist's shop and could not resist buying some. The leaves can be quite large which is useful for filling in spaces in arrangements. It is advisable to obtain some fresh fern so that you can use the leaves as templates and veiners. The leaves are quite a mat green, but can look effective if tinged with gold or silver on the edges.

materials

Mid-holly/ivy flower paste (gum paste)
24-, 22- and 18-gauge wire
Aubergine, dark green, foliage green, moss green and aubergine dusting powders (petal dust/blossom tint)
½ glaze
Gold or silver lustre dust (optional)
Nile green floristry tape

◆

equipment

Fresh fish-tail fern
Sharp scalpel
Sweetcorn husk veiner (optional)
Plain edge cutting wheel [PME]

leaves

1 Roll a ball of well-kneaded, mid-green flower paste into a teardrop shape and flatten. Roll out the shape leaving a thick ridge to insert the wire. (The leaves are quite fine which can make it difficult to insert the wire.)

2 Place a fresh leaf on top of the paste and cut out a leaf using either a scalpel or the cutting wheel. (If the leaves are too large, simply cut them out freehand, following the natural shape of the leaves.) The top edge of each of the leaves should look slightly torn; use a sharp scalpel to cut and flick the edge of each leaf to achieve this effect.

3 Insert a moistened 24- or 22-gauge wire, depending upon the size of the leaf. Pinch the base of the leaf into a sharp point, put it on a pad and soften the edges, trying not to frill the shape.

4 Vein the leaf using the fresh leaf or, alternatively, a sweetcorn husk leaf veiner. Draw a central vein down the fern leaf with the plain edge cutting wheel and then pinch the central vein to accentuate it. The top leaf, which is more of a full fish-tail shape, needs three veins fanning out from the base. Repeat this process to make one central, two medium and two small leaves per stem. Allow the leaves to firm up a little before colouring.

colouring & assembly

5 Dust the edges and the base of each leaf with aubergine dusting powder. Overdust the whole of each leaf with dark green, foliage green and moss green dusting powders. Dip into a ½ glaze and allow to dry. Dust with gold or silver lustre if required.

6 Tape the largest leaf on to the end of an 18-gauge wire using half width nile green floristry tape. Add the two medium leaves together, so that they emerge from the same point, before adding the two smaller leaves.

Christmas Chilli Pepper Cake

It is always very difficult trying to create new themes for Christmas cakes! Last year I bought a bag full of large red and green chillies with the intention of stringing them up around the house as alternative Christmas decorations. Unfortunately, I actually ran out of time and had to resort to the usual trimmings. However, I have at last put my chilli plan into action by using the peppers on this Christmas cake, which makes a stunning contemporary display.

cake & decoration

20cm (8in) long octagonal fruit cake
Apricot glaze
750g (1½lb) white almond paste (marzipan)
Clear alcohol (kirsch, white rum, cointreau etc)
1kg (2lb) white sugarpaste (rolled fondant)
Fine green braid to trim the base of the cake
Red velvet ribbon to trim the edge of the cake board
Non-toxic glue stick
Red, vine green, holly/ivy and forest green dusting powders (petal dust/blossom tint)
Isopropyl alcohol

◆

equipment

Sugarpaste smoothers
30cm (12in) long octagonal cake board
Paintbrushes
Christmas Chilli Pepper Cake template (see p.158)

◆

flowers

2 sprays of chillies with flowers, foliage and fruit (see p.144)

preparation

1 Brush the cake with apricot glaze and cover with a layer of almond paste. If possible, allow the surface to dry – although my Christmas cakes tend to be made at the last minute and so the sugarpaste gets put on top fairly soon after the cake is covered! Moisten the surface of the almond paste with clear alcohol and cover with sugarpaste, using smoothers to create a smooth finish.

2 Cover the cake board with sugarpaste and place the cake on top, making sure that there is a neat join between the cake base and the board.

3 Attach a band of green braid around the base of the cake using a tiny amount of softened sugarpaste. Secure a band of red ribbon to edge of the board using the glue stick.

cake & board design

4 Either paint the design freehand, or use the template supplied on page 158. Use the green and red dusting powders diluted with a small amount of isopropyl alcohol to paint the chillies on to the board and cake surface. Add calyces and stems with a finer brush and dark green dusting powder.

assembly

5 Wire up two stems of chillies with flowers, foliage and fruit, making one about half the size of the other. Position the two stems carefully on the cake, as pictured here.

Exotic Christmas Decorations

It can be wonderful fun to extend the application of sugar flowers to use as table decorations, particularly for special occasions. Chillies are quite simple to make and are not too time consuming, which makes them ideal for Christmas dinner parties where there will be numerous guests! The two arrangements shown here are great to make and will add a very special touch to any festive feast.

Christmas Chilli Peppers
(Capsicum frutescens, C. annum)

Chilli peppers originating from tropical India, Thailand, East and West Africa, and Spain are part of the *Solanaceae* family, which includes the potato, tomato and aubergine. The Christmas chilli pepper has been in cultivation since the middle of the 16th century, although it is not known who first discovered it.

materials

Small white seed-head stamens
28-, 26-, 24- and 20-gauge white wire
Non-toxic high-tack craft glue
Red, vine and forest green, holly/ivy, primrose and aubergine dusting powders (petal dust/blossom tint)
White, poppy red, pale and mid-holly/ivy coloured flower paste (gum paste)
Nile green floristry tape
¼ and full glaze
Scarlet craft dust

equipment

Celstick
Six-petal pointed blossom cutter [OPN6]
Foam pad
Dresden veining tool
Cage or sharp scalpel
Plain edge cutting wheel (optional) [PME]
Bittersweet or physalis leaf veiners [GI]
Ball tool
Fine-nosed pliers
Wire cutters

stamens

1 Glue six short stamens on to the end of a 26-gauge white wire. Allow to dry before dusting the tips with primrose dusting powder.

flower

2 Roll a ball of well-kneaded, white flower paste into a cone shape. Pinch the broad end of the cone to form a pedestal. Roll out the edge of the shape using a celstick, trying to form a neat waistline.

3 Cut out the flower shape using the six-petal pointed blossom cutter. Place the flower on to a pad and soften the edges slightly. Open up the centre of the flower with the pointed end of the

celstick. Place the flower over your index finger and vein each petal using the broad end of the dresden tool. Pinch the tips of each petal into a sharp point. Moisten the base of the dried stamens and pull through the centre of the flower. Thin down the back of the flower and remove any excess paste before allowing to dry.

buds

4 Form a ball of white flower paste into a cone shape. Insert a hooked, moistened 28-gauge wire into the broad end of the cone, and then work the base of the cone down on to the wire to form a tapered back. Divide the point into six sections using either a cage (see page 149 in Equipment and Techniques) or a sharp scalpel.

leaves

5 Roll out some mid-green flower paste, leaving a thick ridge to insert a wire. Cut out a basic leaf shape using a sharp scalpel or cutting wheel. Depending upon the size of the leaf, insert a moistened 26- or 24-gauge wire. Place the leaf on a pad and soften the edges. Vein the leaf with either the bittersweet veiner or physalis veiner (both are from the same family as the chilli). Pinch the leaf from the base to the tip and allow to dry a little before dusting with powder.

6 Dust the leaf with forest green, vine green and holly/ivy dusting powders. Dip into a 1/4 glaze.

7 Tape over each of the leaf, bud and flower stems with half width nile green floristry tape.

chillies

8 Bend a hook in the end of a 24-gauge wire. Form a ball of pale green or poppy red paste into a long, tapered chilli shape, by applying pressure on the paste with your index finger against your palm. Insert a moistened, hooked wire, and then give the chilli a bend. The pale green paste is used to make the smaller, unripened chillies.

calyx

9 Take a small ball of holly/ivy paste and pinch into a cone. Hollow out the broad end using a small ball tool (it looks a bit like an acorn cup at this stage). Moisten the centre and thread on to the back of the chilli. Thin down the base of the calyx on to the wire to elongate it slightly.

colouring & assembly

10 Dust the chillies before they dry in order to achieve strong colours. Dust the green chillies with vine green and holly/ivy and dust some of the larger green chillies with a dash of red or scarlet. Dust the red chillies heavily with

red dusting powder or scarlet craft dust and allow to dry. Dip the peppers into a full glaze. If you require a very high gloss finish, dip the chillies a second time. (This is because the sugar will absorb a certain amount of the glaze, if it is not fully dry.) Dust the calyx with the holly/ivy and forest green dusting powders.

11 Tape the flowers and buds into small groups with the occasional small green chilli added to each. Tape together some single-coloured chilli groups, and some mixed bunches of both red and green. Tape these, together with the leaves on to a piece of 20-gauge wire, using half width nile green tape.

Equipment & Techniques

This basic list of equipment is required to make the sugar flowers and foliage used in the book. Any special pieces of equipment needed to make specific cakes or flowers is listed with each set of instructions. Most of the equipment is available from specialist cake decorating suppliers.

equipment

Board and Rolling Pin

A non-stick board and rolling pin are essential for rolling out flower paste thinly. I prefer to work on a dark green non-stick board, as a white board strains your eyes if you are working for long periods of time. If you are making a lot of flowers and foliage, then you might prefer to use a grooved board or rolling pin to create thick central ridges on petals and leaves to allow the wires to be inserted, rather than using the other method as described in 'techniques' (p.148). These are available commercially, but you can also make grooves yourself in the back of a non-stick board. To do this, heat a metal skewer until it turns red hot, then brand the back of the board several times until you have achieved a groove of the required depth and width. I find that one long groove across the board is most useful, plus a smaller, finer groove at one side of the board. Scrape off any excess plastic, and then smooth the board with some fine glass paper.

Foam Pads

These are used to hold paste while you soften or vein a petal or leaf. There are several pads that are commercially available. If you are planning to buy a pad for the first time, it must be firm and have a fine texture – there are several brands that are too rough and can easily tear the edges of the paste.

Dresden/Veining Tool

My personal favourite is the black dresden/veining tool made by Jem. The fine end is used for drawing veins down the centre of petals, sepals and leaves. The broad end is used to draw veins and to hollow out the edges and centres of petals and leaves. It can also be used to create an effect known as 'double frilling'. This gives a 'ridged look' and is ideal for creating jagged or ragged edges to leaves and petals.

Celsticks

These are available in four sizes: small, medium, large and extra large. One end of each tool is pointed; the other is rounded. The pointed end is used to open up the centres of flowers and can also be used for veining. The rounded end is used like the bone-end tool, but with the advantage of a range of different sized tools for the various sizes of flowers and leaves. The central part of each of the celsticks can also be used as a rolling pin for flowers formed from a pedestal shape. They are also regularly used for rolling thick ridges on paste needed for wired petals and leaves.

Pliers & Wire Cutters

Small, fine-nosed pliers are essential, but a good pair can be costly. However, they are a delight to use and often become invaluable to sugar crafters. They can be purchased from specialist electrical supply shops. Wire cutters are also very useful; either electrical cutters or a pair of heavy duty florist's scissors.

Floristry Tape

Paper floristry tape is available in many colours but I use mainly nile green, white, beige and twig. The tape has a glue in it that is released when the paper is stretched, so it is important to stretch the tape firmly as you tape over a wire.

Florists' Staysoft

This is basically plasticine, but it is sold by florists' suppliers and some cake-decorating shops in long blocks. It is easier to arrange flowers into this medium, as they can be removed and re-arranged if a mistake is made (as the name implies, it stays soft). Blocks of green can also be obtained from good art shops. If you are planning to use this medium, it must be arranged on a container or disc so that it does not come into immediate contact with the cake.

Tape Shredder

This is used to cut lengths of floristry tape into various widths. If you remove one of the blades, you will have a shredder that will cut one half and two quarter width lengths at the same time. The blades are actually razor blades and will need to be replaced occasionally.

Wires

The quality of the wires available varies; it is best to buy A-grade wire, which can be identified by a red spot on the packet. Although it is more expensive, I advise you to use only this wire. I personally now only buy white wire in gauges from 33-gauge (fine) to 24-gauge (thicker), preferring to tape over the wire with nile green tape during the assembly of the flower. There are also stronger wires available from 22-gauge to 14-gauge wire (the higher the number, the finer the wire). These can be covered or uncovered and it doesn't matter which you use. You can also buy very fine silk-covered 36-gauge wire on a reel, which is ideal for very small flowers.

Great Impressions [GI] Veiners

These are double-sided rubber veiners moulded from real flowers and foliage. They add a great deal of realism to flower work. Once you have cut out the leaf or petal and inserted a wire (see right), place the shape into the veiner (the ridge on the paste should fit into the back piece of the veiner). Press the two sides together firmly and then remove the leaf, now veined on both sides to natural perfection. You will need to assess the thickness of paste required for some of the more heavily veined petals and leaves – if you make the paste too fine the veiner may cut through it!

Ceramic Silk Veining Tool [HP]

This tool has veins on the surface; when rolled over the paste it gives a delicate texture. It can also frill the edges of petals, veining them at the same time.

Cutters

There are many different types of cutters available. Cutters speed up the flower-making process and help to add consistency and accuracy to your work. I use mainly metal cutters as these come in a greater variety of shapes and they

can be adjusted with pliers. I also have a large range of plastic cutters, which are ideal for the intricate work involved in foliage. The majority of the cutters used in this book are readily available from most good cake decorating shops. Some cutters however can be difficult to buy and you will need to order these.

Thread

Fine white lace-making cotton thread (Brock 120) is best used for stamens, although some thicker cotton threads can also be useful.

Stamens

There is a vast range of stamens available to the flower maker. I use mainly white stamens, preferring to colour them to the required colour as I need them. I always keep a supply of small white seed-head stamens and some finer white stamens.

Paintbrushes

Good brushes are essential, although they don't necessarily have to be very expensive. They are one of the most important items in a flower-maker's kit. Remember that the final control and accuracy with colouring can make or break your work. Flat brushes are the most useful for dusting flowers and foliage (round brushes are not firm enough to colour accurately with dusting powders). I often use brushes by Robert Simmons called Craft Painters nos. 6 and 8. You will need a good selection of finer brushes for painting fine details on flowers and foliage.

Low Heat Glue Gun

This can be very useful for glueing florists' staysoft or oasis to boards and stands. The glue sticks are fed into the gun and, when the glue is hot, it can be eased through the gun on to the object. Take care not to burn your fingers as you work and do not use the gun for competition pieces.

Non-toxic High-tack Craft Glue

This is a non-toxic glue that is used to glue stamens on to wire. It should not come into immediate contact with the surface of the cakes but is quite safe to use on flowers with wires in them. Again, do not use for competition work.

Non-toxic glue stick

This is a basic glue stick available in most stationery shops and is used for fixing ribbons to cake boards.

techniques

Wiring Leaves and Petals

Roll out some flower paste to the required thickness, leaving a thick ridge down the centre – this can be achieved either by rolling a piece of well-kneaded paste with a large celstick, leaving the centre thicker, or by rolling out the paste on a grooved board. I prefer to use the first method if I have time, as the finished result is often neater and stronger. Cut out the petal or leaf shape using a cutter or template. You will need to position the cutter so that the ridge of paste runs from the tip to the base of the leaf or petal. Press the cutter down firmly, then release the paste from the cutter. (I often find that I end up with cleaner cut edges if I scrub the cutter and paste against the board.) Moisten the end of a wire and insert it into the thick ridge, holding the paste firmly between your finger and thumb to prevent the end of the wire from piercing through. Always insert the wire into at least half the length of the paste ridge. This will ensure that the petal or leaf gets adequate support and is not likely to bend under its own weight.

Colouring

I use a small selection of paste food colourings to colour flower paste, preferring to alter and colour the flowers and foliage with dusting powders (petal dust/blossom tint) after shaping. Powders can also be mixed into flower paste as colouring, but avoid large proportions as they can alter the consistency. I usually colour the paste a paler shade of the colour that I want the finished flower to be, then dust on top to achieve greater depth. It is important to have a good selection of dusting powder colours and to experiment with different colour combinations to obtain the effect you want. I rarely use only one colour on a flower or leaf. The colours can either be mixed together or simply

brushed on to the paste in layers. The instructions for each of the flowers in this book include a list of colours used. I am very fond of green and so most of my cakes have a lot of foliage on them. I usually mix up a large pot of colour in advance, rather than mixing up small amounts at a time, as this wastes both time and dusting powder!

If you want to make a colour paler, it will need to be mixed with white dusting powder. Sometimes a little cornflour (cornstarch) is added, but this is usually to clean the colour out of a brush and to give a very subtle tinge to the petal tips. I use only a few liquid colours, the main one being cyclamen, to paint detail spots and lines on to petals.

Glazing

There are several ways to add a glaze to flowers and leaves; I use only two. The steaming method is used not to give a high gloss, rather to create a 'waxy' finish or, more often, to remove the dry dusted appearance left by dusing powder. It is also used when trying to create a velvety finish or for darkening the depth of colour on a flower or a leaf, since the surface of the paste is still slightly damp after steaming.

Hold each flower or leaf in the steam from a boiling kettle for a few seconds, or until the surface turns shiny. Take great care as too much steam can soften and dissolve the sugar. For a more permanent and shiny glaze, use confectioners' varnish. Used neat (full glaze), this gives a high gloss, which is ideal for berries and glossy leaves. However, for most foliage this looks too artificial, so it is better to dilute the varnish with isopropyl alcohol (available from chemists). Confectioners' varnish is actually made from a base of isopropyl alcohol and shellac. Mix the varnish and alcohol in a lidded container and shake to mix – not too much as this will create tiny air bubbles. The glaze can be used straight away; simply dip the leaf, petal or a group of pieces into the glaze, shake off the excess and dry on absorbent kitchen paper. The glaze may be applied with a paintbrush, but I find the brush strokes tend to remove the colour in streaks. The following glazes are those most often used.

$^1/_4$ glaze

Three-quarters alcohol to a quarter part varnish. This is used for leaves that don't have much shine; the glaze just takes away the flat, dusty look of a leaf or petal.

$^1/_2$ glaze

Equal proportions of alcohol and varnish. This gives a natural shine that is ideal for many foliages, including ivy and rose leaves.

$^3/_4$ glaze

Quarter part alcohol to three-quarters varnish. This gives a semi-gloss without the 'plastic' appearance of a full glaze.

Using a 'Cage'

A wire 'cage' is used to mark the impression of unopened petals on a bud. The 'cage' is made from wire, the gauge depending on the size of the bud. If you are making the bud of a five-petalled flower, you will need five pieces of wire for the 'cage'. Tape the pieces of wire together at one end with half width floristry tape and open up the cage, trying not to cross the wires at the base. Insert the modelled bud, tip or base first, depending on the effect required. Close the wires on to its surface, keeping them as evenly spaced as possible. For some buds, a more realistic effect is achieved if the paste between the wires is pinched out and thinned with your finger and thumb to form a ridge that gives the appearance of larger petals. After removing from the 'cage', twist to give a spiral effect.

Flower Paste

The type of flower paste you use is a matter of personal preference. I prefer a paste that stretches well and does not dry out on the surface too quickly, allowing me to wire petals together whilst they are still damp (a factor that most pastes fail in). I now always buy ready-made flower paste (by mail order) because it is more consistent than home-made paste, and it saves me a lot of time and trouble. Make your own from the following recipe if you wish.

25ml (5 teaspoons) cold water
10ml (2 teaspoons) powdered gelatine
500g (1lb/3 cups) icing (confectioners') sugar, sifted
15ml (3 teaspoons) gum tragacanth
10ml (2 teaspoons) liquid glucose
15ml (3 teaspoons) white vegetable fat (shortening)
1 medium egg white (preferably free-range)

1 Mix the water and gelatine together in a small heatproof bowl and leave to stand for 30 minutes. Sift the icing sugar and gum tragacanth into the bowl of a heavy-duty mixer and mix.

2 Place the bowl with the gelatine mixture over a saucepan of hot water and stir until the gelatine has dissolved. Warm a teaspoon in hot water, then measure out the liquid glucose (the heat should help to ease the glucose off the spoon). Add the glucose and white fat to the gelatine mixture, and continue to heat until all of the ingredients have melted and are thoroughly mixed together.

3 Add the dissolved gelatine mixture to the icing sugar, along with the egg white. Fit the beater to the machine and turn it on at its lowest speed. Beat until mixed, then increase the speed to maximum until the paste becomes white and stringy.

4 Remove the paste from the bowl and rub a thin layer of white fat over it to prevent the outer part drying out. Place in a plastic bag and store in an airtight container. Allow the paste to rest and mature for at least 12 hours before using it.

Working with Flower Paste

You will need a pot of fresh egg white, a pot of cornflour (cornstarch) and white vegetable fat. There has been a trend over recent years to use gum arabic solution, gum glues, water and alcohol as replacements for egg white (because of the salmonella scares). I have continued to use fresh egg white as it is far superior to any of the alternatives.

1 The paste should be kneaded well before it is modelled into a flower or rolled out on a board, otherwise it has a tendency to dry out and crack around the edges. If the paste is dry or tough, then soften it using fresh egg white (not gum arabic etc) – do not add it in large quantities as this will make the paste short, difficult to work with and it will take longer to dry.

2 If the paste is sticky, then a small amount of white fat may be used on the fingers while you knead it – but do not add too much! For many people, there is a temptation to add cornflour (cornstarch) to the paste when it is sticky. However, while cornflour can be used on the surface of the paste quite happily, if it is added to flower paste it seems to aggravate the stickiness.

3 Always grease the board with white fat, then remove almost completely with absorbent kitchen paper. This will form a very thin layer of fat on the board and stop the paste gripping to the board. If you use too much fat it will show up on the finished petal or leaf when you apply dusting powder.

4 Although the commercial paste that I use does not dry out very quickly, it is advisable if you are cutting out a large number of petals to cover them with a celflap or a plastic bag to stop the surface crusting over.

Royal Icing with Dried Albumen

This royal icing recipe is suitable for coating, piping a snail trail, and shells, runouts, brush embroidery etc. It makes about 2kg (4lb) of icing.

45g (3 tablespoons) pure dried albumen powder
315ml (10fl oz/1¼ cups) water
1.75kg (3¼lb/10½ cups) icing (confectioners') sugar, sifted

1 Wash the mixer bowl, a small bowl and the beater with a concentrated detergent and scald to remove any grease and leftover detergent.

2 Reconstitute the dried albumen with the water in a small bowl. It will become very lumpy but continue to stir and then leave it to dissolve for about 20 minutes. Then strain it into the mixer bowl.

3 Add the sifted icing sugar gradually into the albumen. Fix the bowl and beater to the electric mixer and beat on the slowest speed for 4 minutes (soft peak) or 5 minutes (full peak).

Royal Icing (with fresh egg white)

This recipe is intended for fine lace and long extension work, although I have been known to use it for embroidery, snail trail and shells, omitting the tartaric and acetic acids (which are added to the egg white to alter the PH balance).

1 medium egg white
Pinch of tartaric acid
(for fine lace work)
or 2 drops of acetic acid (for long dropped lines of extension work)
225g (8oz/1¾ cups) icing
(confectioners') sugar, sifted

1 Wash and scald the bowl and beater as described before. Place the egg white into the bowl with the pinch of tartaric acid. Add the majority of the icing sugar and mix the two together.

2 Fix the bowl to the machine and beat on the slowest speed until it has reached full peak – about 8 minutes. You may need to mix in some more sugar if the mixture is too soft.

Coating with Sugarpaste

1 Knead the sugarpaste (rolled fondant) to make it smooth try not to knead too many air bubbles into it. Lightly dust the work surface with icing (confectioners') sugar. Roll out the sugarpaste to an even thickness, about 1cm (½in). Moisten the surface of the almond paste with clear alcohol (kirsch, white rum, cointreau etc). Form an even coating of alcohol – if you have dry areas, these will be prone to forming air bubbles with the sugarpaste.

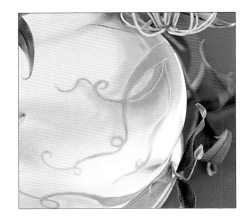

2 Lift the sugarpaste over the cake and ease it into position, smoothing out the top. Trim the sugarpaste from around the base of the cake. Polish the top and the sides using sugarpaste smoothers. I also use a pad of sugarpaste pressed into the palm of my hand to smooth the edges and corners of the cake. If you catch the paste and make an indent, try smoothing it over with the pad of paste.

Covering a Cake Board with Sugarpaste

Moisten the board with a small amount of boiled water or clear alcohol. Roll out sugarpaste to cover the board, trim the edge and soften with the smoother.

note

To prevent the cake and the sugarpaste on the board from becoming sticky, try one of these options. Firstly, you can cut out some sugarpaste from the board, to the same shape and size as that of the cake, and then position the cake on top. Alternatively, place the cake on a thin board of the same size and shape before it is almond-pasted and sugarpasted, then position it on to the larger board.

The Parts of a Flower

Throughout this book, reference is made to the various parts of a flower. These notes will help you identify them.

Pistil

This is the female part of a flower and is made up of a stigma, style and ovary. The pistil varies in its formation between the various different flowers. In some flowers, such as a lily, the pistil can be large.

Stamens

The stamens provide the male part of a flower and are made up of a filament and a pollen-covered anther.

Petals

These are usually the most attractive, coloured parts of a flower; their main purpose being to attract insects.

Tepals

These look like petals and appear in flowers that have no calyx, such as anemone, hellebore or lily.

Calyx and Sepals

The calyx is made up of several individual sepals. It is the outer layer of a bud that protects the flower while it is forming inside.

Bract

This is located where the flower stem joins the main stem. It is a small, modified leaf (intermediate between the sepals and the leaves).

Spadix

This is a fleshy axis that carries both male and female flowers, such as the centre of an arum lily or anthurium.

Spathe

This is a large petal-like bract that is usually wrapped around or positioned below the spadix of the arum lily and anthurium.

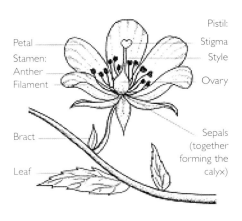

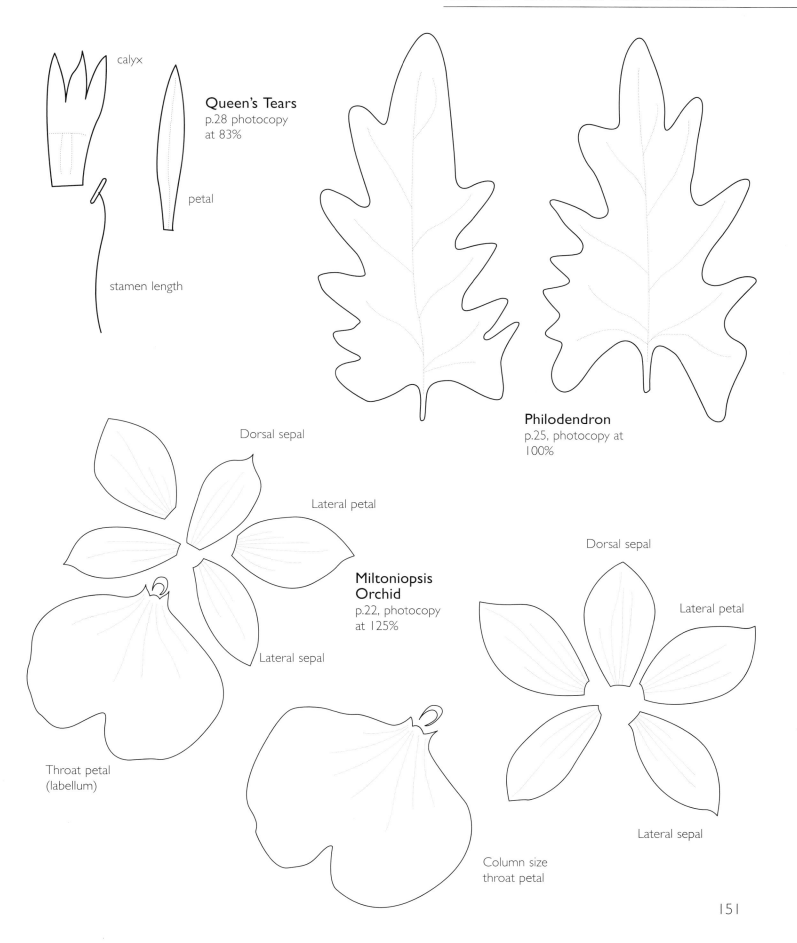

calyx

Queen's Tears
p.28 photocopy
at 83%

petal

stamen length

Philodendron
p.25, photocopy at
100%

Dorsal sepal

Lateral petal

**Miltoniopsis
Orchid**
p.22, photocopy
at 125%

Lateral sepal

Dorsal sepal

Lateral petal

Throat petal
(labellum)

Lateral sepal

Column size
throat petal

Stamen/petal

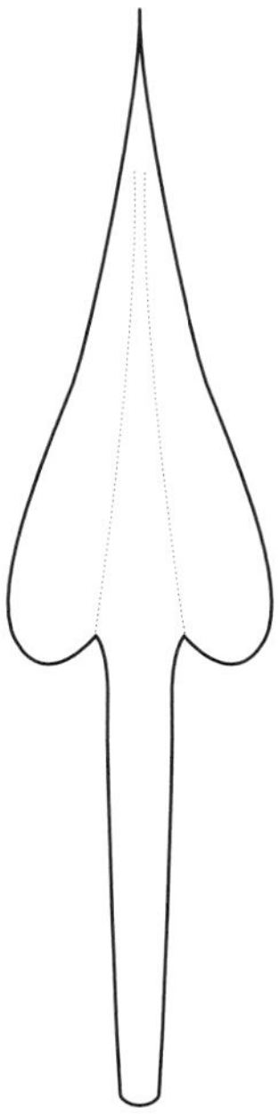

Stamen/bract

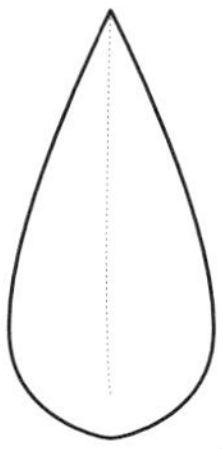

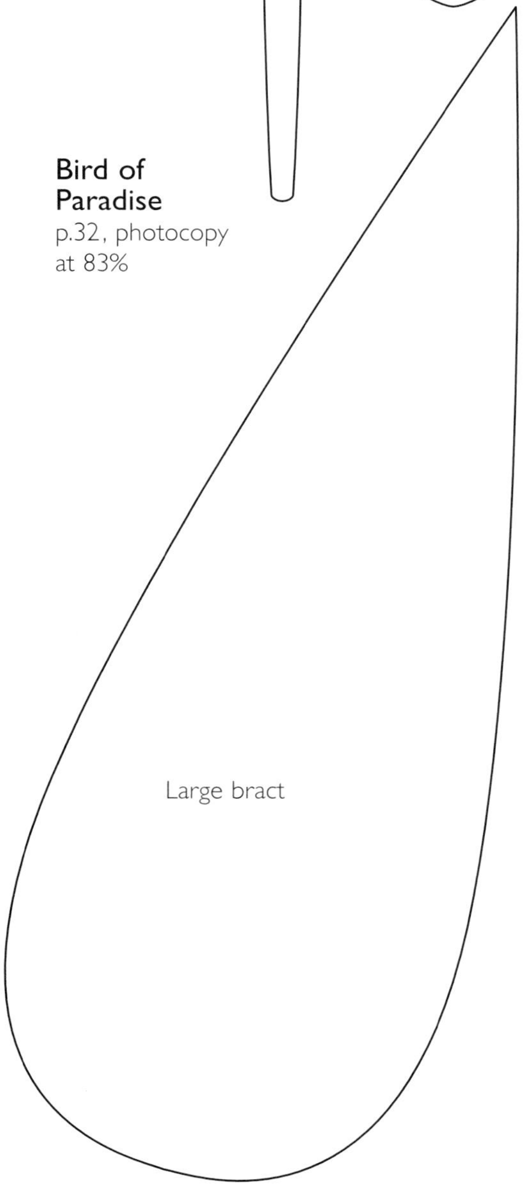

Bird of Paradise
p.32, photocopy at 83%

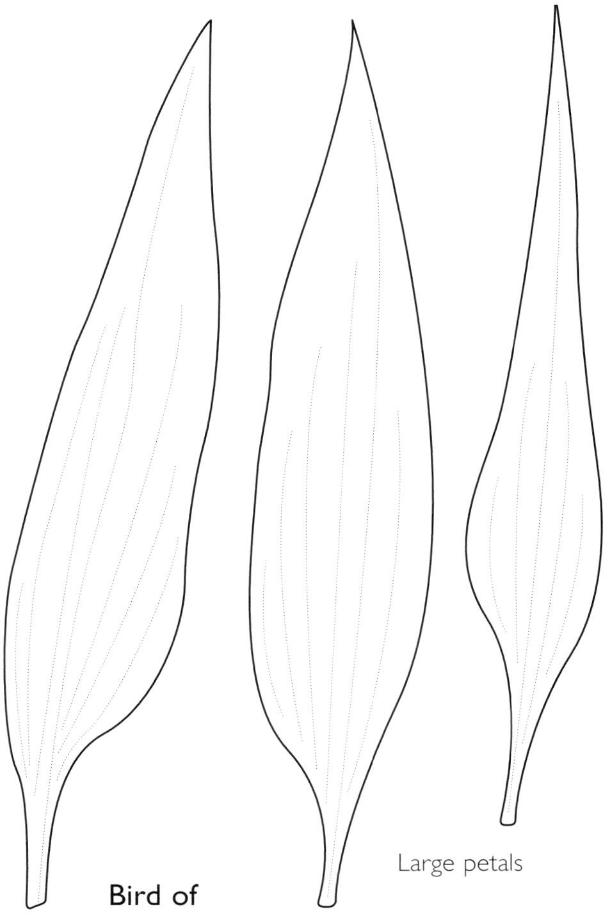

Large bract

Bird of Paradise
p.32, photocopy at 100%

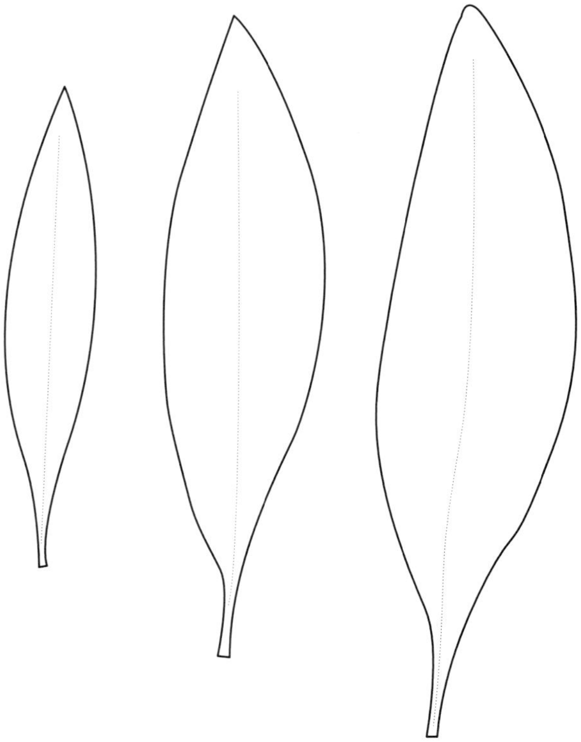

Large petals

South Sea Island Ti Leaf
p.26, photocopy at 100%

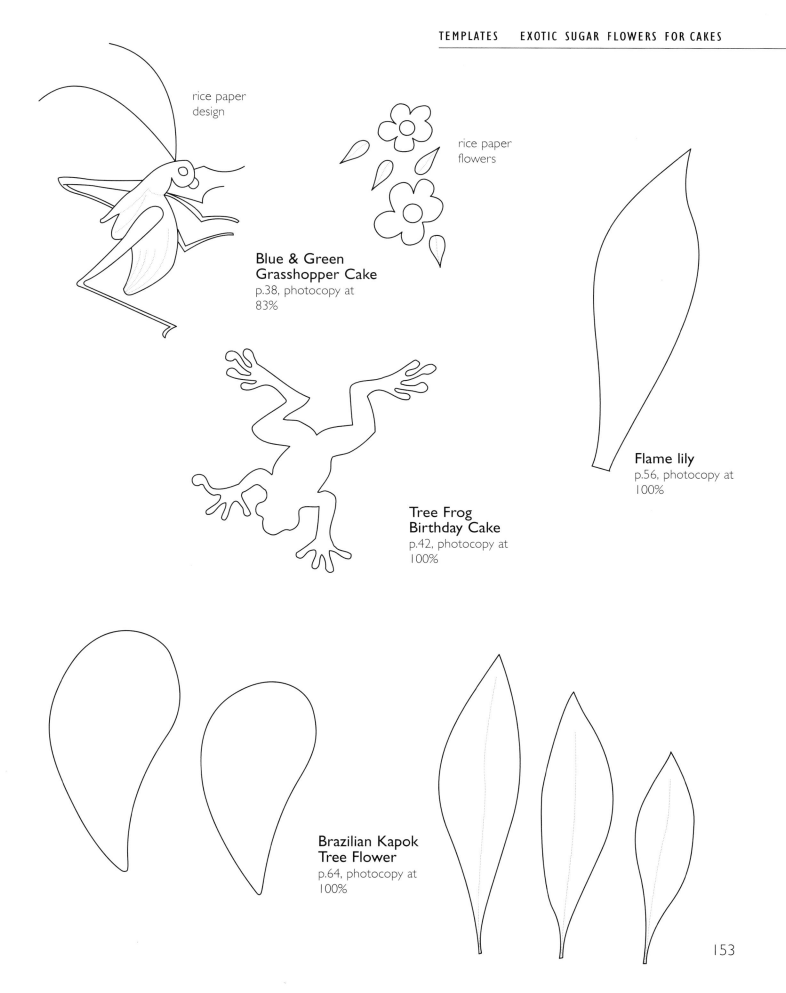

rice paper
design

rice paper
flowers

**Blue & Green
Grasshopper Cake**
p.38, photocopy at
83%

**Tree Frog
Birthday Cake**
p.42, photocopy at
100%

Flame lily
p.56, photocopy at
100%

**Brazilian Kapok
Tree Flower**
p.64, photocopy at
100%

153

Petals

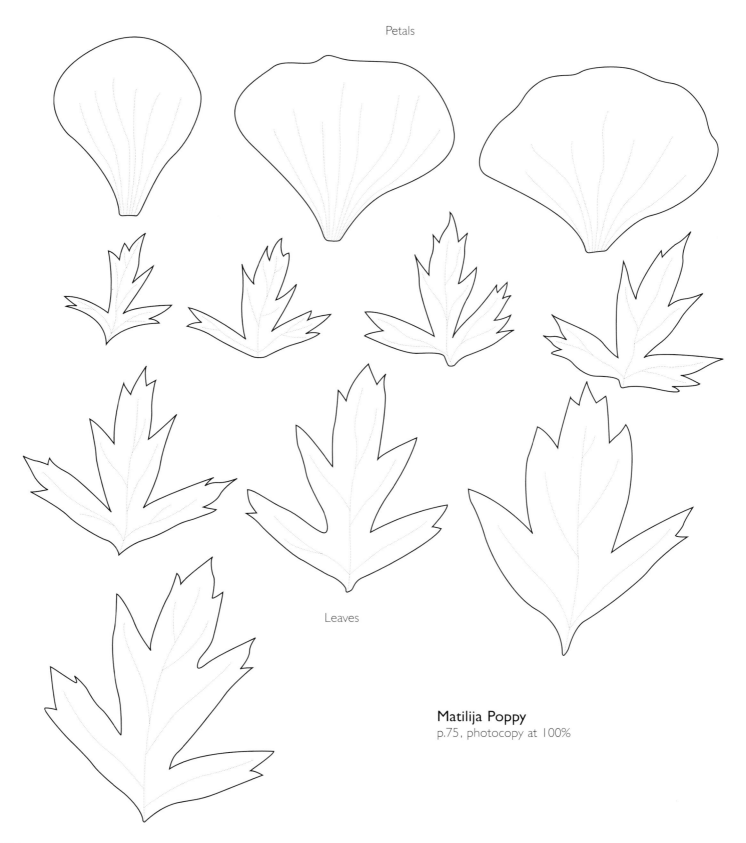

Leaves

Matilija Poppy
p.75, photocopy at 100%

Single peony leaves

Single Peony
p76, photocopy
at 100%

Single peony petals

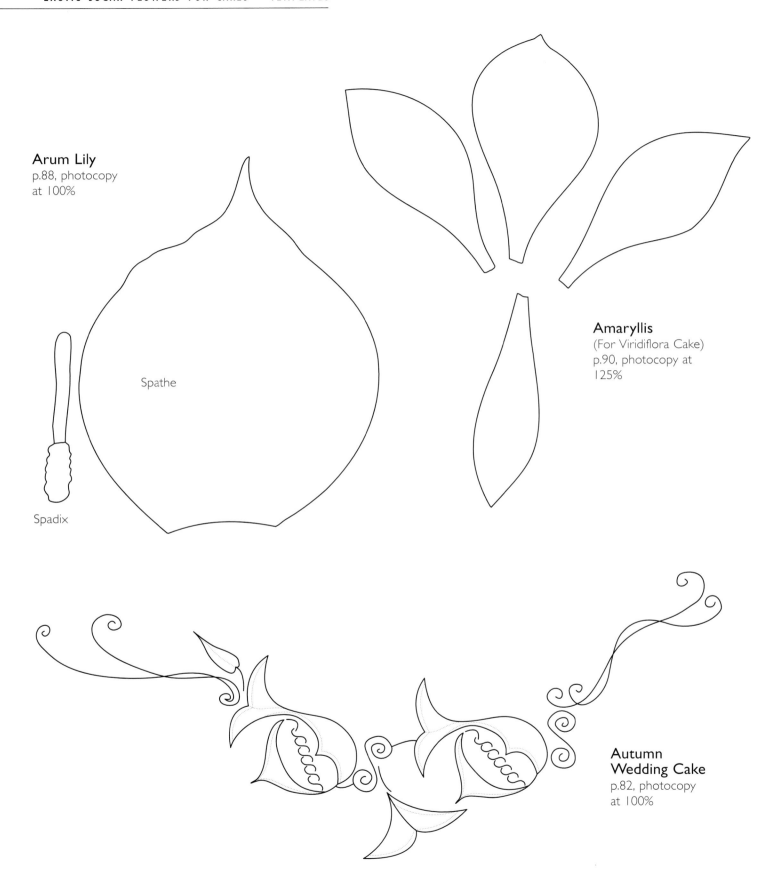

Arum Lily
p.88, photocopy
at 100%

Spathe

Spadix

Amaryllis
(For Viridiflora Cake)
p.90, photocopy at
125%

**Autumn
Wedding Cake**
p.82, photocopy
at 100%

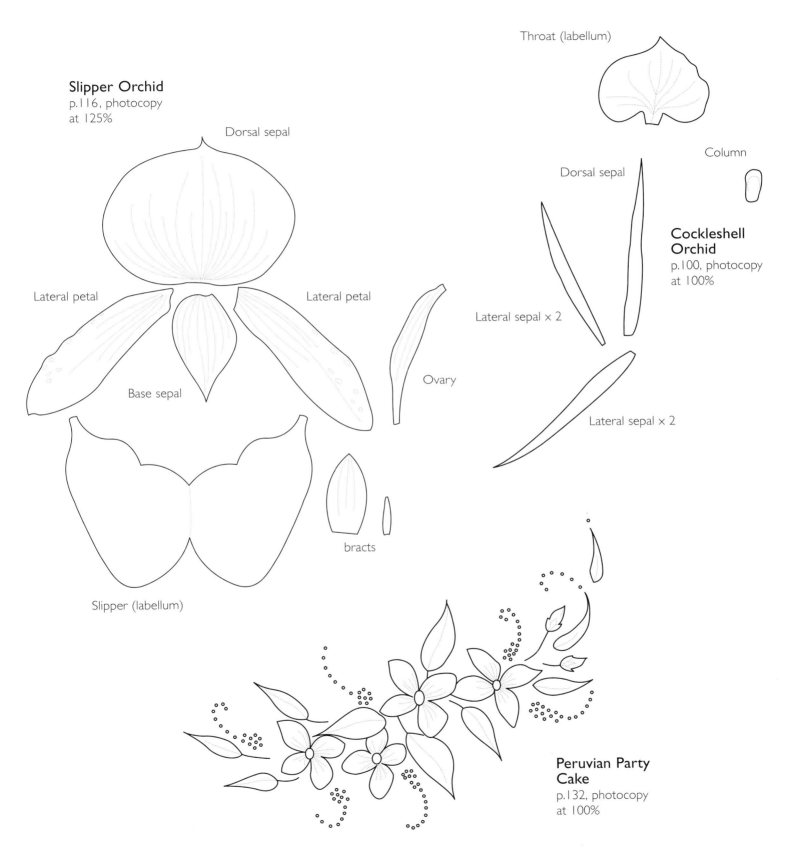

Throat (labellum)

Slipper Orchid
p.116, photocopy
at 125%

Dorsal sepal

Column

Dorsal sepal

Cockleshell
Orchid
p.100, photocopy
at 100%

Lateral petal   Lateral petal

Lateral sepal × 2

Base sepal

Ovary

Lateral sepal × 2

bracts

Slipper (labellum)

Peruvian Party
Cake
p.132, photocopy
at 100%

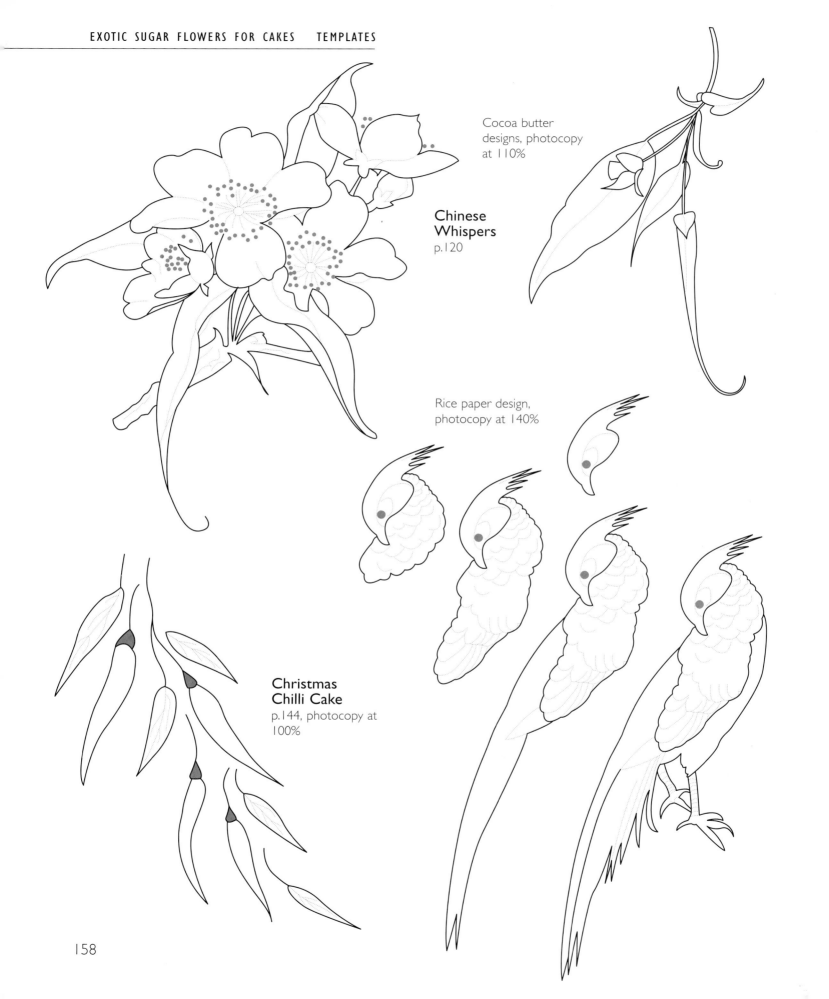

Cocoa butter
designs, photocopy
at 110%

**Chinese
Whispers**
p.120

Rice paper design,
photocopy at 140%

**Christmas
Chilli Cake**
p.144, photocopy at
100%

Index

Published in 2000 by Merehurst Limited, Ferry House, 51–57 Lacy Road, Putney, London, SW15 1PR

ISBN 1 85391 802 4

© Merehurst Limited 2000

All rights reserved. No part of this publication may be reproduced, stored on a retrieval system or transmitted in any form or by any means, electronic, mechanical, photocopying, recording or otherwise, without prior written permission of the copyright owner and the publisher of this book.

A catalogue record for this book is available from the British Library.

Commissioning Editor:
Barbara Croxford
Project Editor:
Angela Newton
Editorial Assistance:
Sarah Wilde, Sarah Widdecombe and Sarah Harley
Design:
Cathy Lazell and Wladek Szechter
Publishing Manager:
Fia Fornari
Production Manager:
Lucy Byrne
CEO & Publisher:
Anne Wilson
Marketing & Sales Director:
Kathryn Harvey
International Sales Director:
Kevin Lagden

Photography by: Sue Atkinson
Templates by: Chris King

Colour separation by: Colourscan
Printed by: Tien Wah Press in Singapore

Other Merehurst books by Alan Dunn:

Floral Wedding Cakes & Sprays
Sugar Flowers for All Seasons
Wild Flowers (Sugar Inspirations series)

Acknowledgements & Suppliers

Acknowledgements

There have been moments when I thought that this book would never be finished! My sincere thanks go to those people who have encouraged, supported and had faith in me. You helped to spur me on. Without your help, you would not be reading this now!

Thank you Alice (my Northern Star!) for your never-ending help which came in so many forms. It was invaluable in the production of this book! To Tombi Peck for kindly donating your proteas, and for your help during the midnight hours! Thank you Maria Harrison for your patience and many organising skills.

I would also like to thank Sarah and Danny Pace, and Jean and Steven Folan, for allowing your wedding cakes to be featured in this book.

Thanks also go to Peter Stott, Tony Warren, Viv Soulsby, Stephanie Scott and Alison Ruaux for your help and advice. I would like to thank Jill Draper and Mrs Higginbotham for providing me with the necessary bilbergia plants. Thank you Rosie Peck, Peggie Green and Conor Day for accommodation during the writing of this book.

Thank you to Renshaw Scott for supplying Regalice, Norma Laver and Jenny Walker at 'A Piece of Cake' for your superb flower paste and kind hearts. I would like to thank Joan Mooney of 'Great Impressions' for supplying most of the rubber veiners used in this book. Thank you Beverley and Rob Dutton of 'Squires Kitchen' for the large pots of dusting powder, to Marion Holmes at 'Cakes, Classes and Cutters' for sorting out the dummies.

I would like to thank Barbara Croxford, my commissioning editor, for all your help and patience, and to Sue Atkinson for your wonderful expertise with the camera, and for your quirky sense of humour.

Thanks, finally, to Joni Mitchell and Shawn Colvin for your musical company during long, creative sessions.

Sugarcraft Suppliers

A Piece of Cake
18 Upper High Street
Thame, Oxon
OX9 3EX
tel./fax. 0184 421 3428

Cakes, Classes and Cutters
23 Princes Road
Brunton Park, Gosforth
Newcastle-Upon-Tyne
NE3 5TT
tel./fax. 0191 217 0538

Celcakes and Celcrafts [C]
Springfield House
Gate Helmsley, York,
Yorkshire, TO4 1NF
tel./fax. 01759 371 447

Confectionery Supplies
3 Lower Cathedral Road
Cardiff, Gwent
tel. 01222 372 1610

Cooks Corner
35 Percy Street
Newcastle-Upon-Tyne
Tyne & Wear
tel. 0191 261 5481

Country Cutters [CC]
Lower Tresauldu
Dingestow, Monmouth,
Gwent, NP5 4BQ
tel. 01600 740448

Creating Cakes
The Cake Decorating Centre
63 East Street, Sittingbourne
Kent, ME10 4BQ
tel. 01795 426358

Culpitt Cake Art, Culpitt Ltd
Jubilee Industrial Estate
Ashington, Northumberland,
NE63 8UQ
tel. 01670 814 545

Fleurtatious (Flower shop)
58 Acorn Road, Jesmond
Newcastle-Upon-Tyne
Tyne & Wear
tel. 0191 281 3127

Great Impressions [GI]
14 Studley Drive
Swarland, Northumberland
NE65 9JT
tel./fax. 01670 787 061

Guy, Paul and Co. Ltd
Unit B4, Foundry Way
Little End Road
Eaton Socon
Cambs, PE19 3JH

Holly Products [HP]
Holly Cottage
Hassall Green, Cheshire
CW11 4YA
tel./fax. 01270 761 403

Orchard Products [OPR]
51 Hallyburton Road
Hove, East Sussex
BN3 7GP
tel. 01273 419418
fax. 01273 412512

Renshaw Scott Ltd
Crown Street
Liverpool, L8 7RF
tel. 0151 706 8200

W. Robertson (Billy's Blocks)
The Brambles, Ryton,
Tyne & Wear, NE40 3AN
tel. 0191 413 8144

Squires Kitchen [SK]
Squires House,
3 Waverley Lane
Farnham, Surrey
GU9 8BB
tel. 01252 711749
fax. 01252 714714

Sugar Celebrations
37 Faringdon Road
Swindon, Wiltshire
SN1 5AR
tel./fax. 01793 513 549

The British Sugarcraft Guild
National Office
Wellington House
Messeter Place, Eltham,
London, SE9 5DP
tel. 020 8859 6943
fax. 020 8859 6117

The Flower Basket
10 High Street
Much Wenlock
Shropshire
tel. 01952 728 101

The Old Bakery
Kingston St Mary
Taunton, Somerset
TA2 8HW
tel./fax. 01823 451205

The Secret Garden
(flower shop)
17 Clayton Road
Jesmond, Tyne & Wear
tel. 0191 281 7753

The Stencil Library [TSL]
Stocksfield Hall
Stocksfield
Northumberland

Tinkertech Two [TT]
(Metal cutters)
40 Langdon Road
Parkstone, Poole
Dorset, BH14 9EH
tel. 01202 738 049

Non-UK

Beryl's Cake Decorating
& Pastry Supplies
P.O.Box 1584
N. Springfield
VA22151–0584, USA
tel. + 1 800 488 2749

Cakes & Co.
25 Rock Hill
Blackrock Village
Co. Dublin, Ireland
tel. + 353 1 283 6544

The Cake Decorating Centre
1 Adelaide Arcade
Adelaide
South Australia 5000
tel. + 61 8 8223 1719

Cake Decorators' Supplies
Shop 1,
770 George Street
Sydney 2001
Australia
tel. + 61 2 9212 4050

Elegant Cutwork Collection
1007 Lochmore Blvd
Grosse Ptd Woods
NJ 48236, USA

The European Cake Gallery
844 North Crowley Road,
Crowley,
Texas
76036 USA
tel. + 817 297 2240